Leaders Learning to Listen

Leaders Learning to Listen

Chris Edmondson

DARTON · LONGMAN + TODD

First published in 2010 by
Darton, Longman and Todd Ltd
1 Spencer Court
140 – 142 Wandsworth High Street
London SW18 4JJ

ISBN: 978-0-232-52736-0

A catalogue record for this book is available from the British Library

Phototypeset by Kerrypress Ltd, Luton, Bedfordshire
Printed and bound in Great Britain by CPI Antony Rowe, Chippenham

Contents

To all those who over the years have offered me the hospitality of true listening, especially Father Simon Holden CR, and those whom I now serve as Bishop.

Acknowledgements

The roots of this book go back to my time as Warden of the Lee Abbey Community and Conference Centre in North Devon (2002–2008). As part of the conference and retreat programme, a number of us in the community would regularly offer workshops on a variety of subjects. One that I began to lead was simply entitled 'Listening to God'. It was always well subscribed, and together gave us the opportunity of recognising that God is 'speaking' far more than we often realise, as well as identifying some of the barriers that can prevent us 'hearing'.

Recognising that an hour was far too short to do justice to the immensely important but often neglected subject, I was encouraged to offer this listening theme as the subject for a whole conference.

As is often the case for those of us who preach and teach, I gained as much if not more than the participants, both through the preparation and the delivery of the various sessions. Once again, feedback was very positive, so much so that several of the participants, many of whom were church leaders, encouraged me to think about writing something that would particularly help people like them in their roles and responsibilities.

Conscious that many other authors had written far more eloquently than I could on the subject of listening, I initially hesitated to follow this up. However, having been given a month's study leave, I resolved to use the time to see if there was scope for a book that would encourage leaders to learn to listen better, for their own wellbeing, as well as helping them navigate some of the challenges and opportunities of leadership in the twenty-first century church, where life can often be so frenetic and driven.

Having done some initial preparatory work, and as a result of being encouraged by the staff at DLT, who had been my publishers before, that I should continue writing, I agreed to sign a contract. Little did I know that a week later I would be invited to come for interview for the post of Bishop of Bolton within the Diocese of Manchester! This left me with a significant challenge of continuing and completing what I had begun, having moved to a new area, and with a significant new responsibility as a bishop. Would this leader have time to write when there was so much else to learn and do? Would he be making time to listen, amongst all the demands, expectations and opportunities that being a bishop brings?

It hasn't been easy, but in another way the commitment to writing this book has helped to ensure that not only in theory, but practice, I have tried to make listening to God and to others a priority in my calling as a bishop.

I am grateful to that end to my friend and colleague Nigel McCulloch, Bishop of Manchester, for encouraging me to make time to complete what I had started. Also to present colleagues in the Bishop's Leadership Team, who have in different ways offered their suggestions and support.

The research for, and writing up of, this book has been greatly helped by those who have offered hospitality to me at different stages in the process. In particular my thanks go to the Lee Abbey, Scargill and Northumbria communities, all of whom in different ways hold a special place in my heart. Also to the staff of the Church of the Nazarene College in Manchester, who have generously made their library facilities available to me. To friends from my time as vicar of St Peter's, Shipley, in the Diocese of Bradford – in particular Bob and Suzanne Evans and Andree Freeman – who at different times gave me space in their homes, enabling me to write undisturbed.

As always my family – who recognise I have still got some way to go in my listening! – have been the source of loving and loyal support. Thank you to my wife Susan, to Martin and Anna, Tim and Jackie.

Finally, my warmest thanks go to my commissioning editor Virginia Hearn at DLT, for believing in the potential of *Leaders Learning to Listen*, and understanding a need to be flexible about deadlines!

As a musician, I found the following comment I read pertinent to the subject of this book: 'The Master is still playing, but listening is optional'. My hope and prayer is that this book may play some small part in enabling leaders in their listening to God, the church and the world, so that they realise that listening is optional but vital for them for their own well-being, and the effectiveness and fruitfulness of their ministries.

Chris Edmondson (Feast of St Barnabas, June 2010)

Introduction

To paraphrase the well-known phrase from Ecclesiastes 12, 'of the making of many books *on listening to God* (my italics), there is no end'! So why another one, when many writers far better 'qualified' than me have offered significant contributions in this area? The answer lies in the first word of the title – 'Leaders' – and again there is arguably an excess of books on leadership, but I would suggest that there is room for something to be written that brings 'leaders and listening' together under one roof.

To continue the questions – what's so special about *leaders* learning to listen? In one sense – nothing. Leadership is one calling among many in the Church, not intrinsically more important than any other calling or area of ministry. And yet there is something within the spiritual gift of leadership (Rom. 12:8), as it involves responsibility for others, that makes it vital that listening for 'the sounds of God' (to use a phrase coined by Michael Mitton) happens. In reality, however, this often gets squeezed out. I know this both from my own experience of nearly forty years in church leadership, and my conversations with others who hold various kinds of leadership responsibilities.

As we will explore in the chapters that follow, there are many reasons why this is the case, and in what follows I will examine in more detail some of the particular factors that make good listening both a challenge and a necessity for the twenty-first century church leader. Whatever else I still have to learn in this area – and there is plenty! – there are two things I know for sure. One is that our capacity as leaders to listen, in whatever area, is in proportion to how well we have been listened to and heard by others. If this has not been our experience, we will find it all the harder to listen in the different contexts this book explores. For example, in her inspirational book *Time to Think*[1], Nancy Kline argues that good decision-making comes from good thinking, and good thinking is a result of being listened to well.

Secondly, as former Archbishop of Canterbury, Donald Coggan, has expressed it:

> Christians believe in a God who speaks. Ours is not a silent God, a God who sits, Sphinx-like, looking out unblinking on a world in agony … He speaks because he loves. Love always seeks to communicate.[2]

That communication happens, as the writer to the Hebrews put it, 'in many and various ways' (Heb. 1.1), and central to the leader's calling is to seek to understand the nature of that speaking both for themselves and those for whom they have responsibility. But as the Western Church, with notable exceptions, experiences a decline in influence and numbers, and potential further division as a result of different theological and ecclesiological perspectives, I want to ask what time and space is being given in our various church councils and synods to hear 'what the Spirit is saying to the churches'? We seem to be awash with ideas and strategies to stem, if not turn, the tide. Some of them undoubtedly have emerged out of good listening – to God, to one another in the Church and the wider context of change in which we find ourselves. But it often seems that listening – in all its forms – is what least characterises church life and leadership. No wonder years ago the novelist E. M. Forster coined the phrase 'poor talkative little Christianity'!

It is my conviction that, if we dare – and it will take courage – as leaders to model and encourage a climate of listening, it will not necessarily be the panacea for all ills, but it could make a significant difference to our fruitfulness and effectiveness as Christians and the Church.

Having referred to some words from a former Archbishop of Canterbury, this is what the current Archbishop, Rowan Williams, had to say, speaking at the 2005 Foundation for Church Leadership Conference:

> For me, part of the burden, the excitement and the challenge of trying to exercise leadership in the Church, is trying to feel the rhythm or the heartbeat of the body of Christ, so that leadership that matters or is effective in the Church, has to be *listening* (italics mine) ... Listening is actually inevitable and built into the structure of Christian leadership ... You must listen to what is actually going on so that when things change or things move, it is the Body, not a group that is coerced or manipulated into following an agenda. So, if it is about following the direction of the Son of God, exercised in listening for what I've called the heartbeat of the body of Christ, it is fairly risky because it's bound to have a rather long vision.[3]

I have discovered there are no short cuts to discerning that 'rhythm and heartbeat' for the Church! It requires those in leadership to answer the kind of question that Henri Nouwen posed towards the end of the last century:

> The central question is, Are the leaders of the future truly men and women of God, people with an ardent desire to dwell in God's presence, to listen to God's voice, to look at God's beauty, to touch God's incarnate Word and to taste fully God's infinite goodness?[4]

I hope that what follows might contribute something to this vital process of leaders learning to listen.

Chapter one

What is listening, and why it is so important for leaders?

I was ordained into the Church of England in 1973, and the theological training I received was substantially the same as my father had experienced some thirty years before. The 1960s had come and gone with all their associated ferment in society. Within the Church, books like John Robinson's *Honest to God* had rattled a number of ecclesiastical cages. But there were still sufficient familiar landmarks and evidences of 'residual Christianity' around, so that the urgency to think about and train people in new ways for leadership in the Church simply was not there. This period was the tail end of what is usually termed now the 'modern' era. 'Postmodernity' was at that stage a word found only on the lips or in the books of a few academics, who were waking up to the significance of the seismic shift in society that would come to affect us all. Leading a changing church in a fast-changing world was not a core part of the curriculum in my ministerial formation. It seems to me that, as a Church, we have been trying to play 'catch-up' ever since.

Writing in the July 2001 edition of the magazine *Quadrant*, Eddie Gibbs, an Anglican priest, and for many years Professor of Church Growth at the USA's Fuller Theological Seminary, sums things up like this:

> We now have a generation of leaders who do not know how to lead within a context of rapid and chaotic change. We were trained to map read on well-marked roads, not navigate on stormy seas. I believe the changes are significant and irreversible – while tomorrow continues to arrive ahead of schedule, yesterday can never be revisited.

One of the books which had a profound impact on me when it was first published in England in 1982, and to which I have returned many times since, is *Christianity Rediscovered – An Epistle from the Masai*, by Vincent Donovan[1]. Donovan was an American Roman Catholic priest who worked for eleven years among the Masai people of Tanzania. In this truly prophetic book, we find someone who realised that the 'old' inherited ways of engaging in mission and ministry were neither being effective, nor were they truly 'Gospel'. Convinced that the existing missionary structures of the Church were doing everything but bringing people to God, he took the considerable risk of working among the Masai, without schools, hospitals, buildings and other 'conventional' resources. He assumed no preconceived notions about God, Christ, salvation, the Church or anything else traditionally associated with Christianity. Instead, going as Jesus had instructed the seventy (Luke 10:1–11), he went empty-handed except for his faith, to visit the Masai people where they were, and especially built relationships over weeks and months with their leaders.

The results of this approach are described in the book with vividness and moving simplicity, as he shares not only the literal physical journeys he made, but the inner journey of discovery, at the heart of which was a commitment to *listening* – to God and to the people. As the story unfolds, it is evident that through this 'double-listening' Donovan was deeply challenged and enabled to cut through many Western Christian assumptions, as he sought, having listened, to make Christ relevant to the Masai, through their own lifestyle, language and culture.

Following that experience, Donovan was called back to work in the USA, and, having been away for a number of years, one of the things that struck him was the alienation of most young people from the church. What seemed especially significant was the way in which, despite so many cultural differences, they reminded him of the groups of young Masai warriors, with their own symbols and values. Also in common was their equally limited understanding of the Christian Gospel. This led Donovan, just as he had asked questions of the Masai tribal leaders, to ask these University students how he could enable the Christian Gospel to make sense to them. One young man gave him this advice, which I would suggest is important for us all to hear: 'Do not try to call them back to where they were. Do not call them to where you are, beautiful as that place may seem to you. You must have the courage to go to a place where neither you nor they have ever been before.'

It has always been important that leaders learn to listen, but it is surely never more so than at significant times of transition and change. Thankfully, in recent years there is evidence of new approaches to training for ministry, that are taking into account this rapidly changing context in which we find ourselves. Even so, as Brian Maclaren commented in an address he gave to the 2008 Lambeth Conference of Bishops, we have to realise that: 'Yesterday's maps are outdated, and today's will soon be too.'

UNDERSTANDING THE MEANING OF LISTENING

Before we look at how those in leadership not only respond to these times of transition, but try to 'get ahead of the game', it is important to be clear what is meant by listening, and what the Bible has to say about its importance, particularly as far as leaders are concerned.

According to the *Oxford Dictionary*, to listen is 'to hear attentively, to give ear, to make an effort to hear something'.

The *Chambers Dictionary* offers similar insights: 'to attempt to hear something or pay attention; to follow advice'.

In these definitions, it is clear that some conscious commitment is required on our part if we are to truly understand, embrace and practice the art of listening. This applies first to intentionally setting aside times of quietness, in order to seek to hear what God may be saying from within that stillness (this will be explored further in the later chapter 'Silence for the leader – friend or foe?'). That commitment is equally vital as we listen to others, where the challenge is to listen without interruption, and to do so with delight and attentiveness. No wonder the Danish philosopher, Soren Kierkegaard, once commented: 'Hearing is the most spiritual of our senses'[2].

LISTENING AND HEARING IN THE BIBLE

When it comes to the principles and practice of listening and hearing in the Bible, it is fascinating to discover that *Cruden's Complete Concordance* has four full pages citing biblical references to 'hearing' and 'listening', and two pages on the word 'voice'[3]. In total, one or other of these two words occurs either in Hebrew or Greek more than 1,500 times. Furthermore, 'hearing' is referred to no less than ninety-one times in the first five books of the Old Testament. It is the patriarch Abraham who is the first recorded 'listener' to God's voice. He appears as the first of many leaders whom we meet in the Old and New Testaments to experience and demonstrate the importance of listening. Alongside that, we note that the first reference to the 'voice of the Lord' being heard comes in Genesis 3:8, and the last in Revelation 22:17.

The following examples, drawn deliberately from different parts of the Old and New Testaments, underline the importance, for the whole people of God, not just their leaders, of the principle of listening:

'Give ears and come to me; listen, so that you might live.'(Isa. 55:3)

'He (God) wakens me morning by morning, wakens my ear to listen like one being taught.' (Isa. 50:4)

'Speak Lord, for your servant is listening.' (1 Sam. 3:10)

Today, if you hear his voice, do not harden your hearts. (Ps. 95:7–8)

'This is my Son, whom I have chosen; listen to him.' (Luke 9:35)

Then Jesus said, 'Whoever has ears to hear, let them hear.' (Mark 4:9)

'I will show you what the person is like who comes to me and hears my words and puts them into practice.' (Luke 6:47)

Now an angel of the Lord said to Philip, 'Go south to the road, the desert road – that goes from Jerusalem to Gaza.' So he started out … (Acts 8:26–27)

We must pay more careful attention, therefore to what we have heard, so that we do not drift away. (Heb. 2:1)

'Whoever has ears to hear, let them hear what the Spirit says to the churches.' (Rev. 2:7)

It is hardly surprising that we find so many references to listening, because the Bible begins with the description of God speaking creation and life itself into being. Both Judaism and Christianity are 'religions of the word', mouth to ear – literally and metaphorically. They are deeply rooted in the aural. Nowhere is that clearer than in the words precious to both Christians and Jews, known as the Shema, words first uttered by Moses, and centuries later re-iterated by Jesus:

'HEAR O Israel: The Lord is our God, the Lord alone. You shall love the Lord your God with all your heart, and with all your soul and with all your might.' (Deut. 6:4–5)

The message here for all God's people, but especially those who are leaders, is to learn to listen to God so we can love him more deeply and love others more completely. If that is God's ultimate design for humanity, that love will only develop through a commitment to learning to listen to God. Listening and loving are always intimately connected.

LEVELS OF LISTENING

What is also clear from the biblical record is that a true understanding of listening is intended to lead to a response of obedience, whether the communication from God has come through an audible voice, dreams and visions, the miraculous, the prophetic or by some other means. The writer to the Hebrews gives us an important reminder, when he describes God as one who speaks in 'many and various ways' (Heb. 1:1). To further underline the importance of response, it is significant that our English word for 'obedience' is derived from two Latin words – *ob* and *audire* – which mean to 'listen keenly'.

As Bill Kirkpatrick observes in his book *The Creativity of Listening,* listening has three meanings:

> The first is to hear; the second is like the meaning of the French 'connaitre' – to understand; and the third is the command to pay attention. In the religious life, obedience is listening.[4]

Another way of understanding what we might describe as this 'listening obedience' that I have found helpful, is by means of focusing on the words 'attention', 'absorption' and 'action'. Attention starts the process of opening our ears: 'Hear, O Israel'. The next level of 'absorption' is well-illustrated also from the Old Testament by Solomon's remarkable request soon after he became King: 'Give your servant therefore an understanding mind' (1 Kings 3:9), or, as it could be translated: 'Give your servant a "hearing" heart'.

A few verses later we are told that God did give him a 'wise and discerning mind' (1 Kings 3:12), one that fully absorbed what he sensed God was saying.

The third level moves from absorption to action, as Jesus was to make clear at the end of his teaching in the Sermon on the Mount:'Everyone then who hears these words of mine and *acts* on them will be like a wise man …' (Matt. 7:24). Or, as we have already noted, when the voice comes from heaven to the disciples of Jesus when he was transfigured: 'Listen to him!' (Luke 9:35).

BIBLICAL LEADERS WHO LISTENED

On many occasions in both Old and New Testaments, we see the outworking of this principle – people whom God called into various kinds of leadership role listening to God and obeying him, often at some cost to themselves, but which ultimately, if not immediately, leads to blessing and fruitfulness.

Starting with the Old Testament, individuals such as Noah, Abraham, Joseph, Moses, Joshua, Elijah, Gideon, David and Josiah, along with the major and minor prophets, bear testimony to this. In particular, I would suggest that the experience of the prophet Daniel connects with some of the challenges leaders face today. Here was someone living and working in an alien and spiritually-diverse culture. He was, with his people, in exile, far away from all that was familiar. At the heart of the book of Daniel is the account of the dream experienced by Nebuchadnezzar, the King of Persia – a dream he was unable to understand. Furthermore, his local magicians, sorcerers and enchanters were no help. However, because of his commitment and openness to God, Daniel was able to interpret the dream, to discern and pass on what God was saying. As the story unfolds, the cost to him becomes clear, but is a pointer to one of the key roles of the leader in every generation – in various ways to listen and interpret for others what God may be saying. That said, the obedience of these and other characters from the Old Testament, like ours, was sometimes reluctant, often faltering, and, on occasions, they too found it hard to move from attention to the levels of absorption and action.

Moving into the New Testament, according to St. Luke's Gospel, the disciples who would become the pioneer leaders of the Church first heard and responded to the call of Christ to 'rise up and follow', as the hymn 'Dear Lord and Father of mankind' puts it, on the shores of Lake Galilee. As the story of Jesus' earthly ministry closes, after the resurrection, those same men heard Jesus tell them to 'wait in the city until you have been clothed with power from on high' (Luke 24:49). There, along with others, they waited, listened and prayed in the Upper Room, until ten days later, 'when the day of Pentecost was fully come, the Holy Spirit was poured out on them all' (Acts 2:4).

In the pages of the Acts of the Apostles that follow, we find example after example of God speaking, in 'many and various ways', and those with leadership responsibilities slowly and sometimes hesitatingly learning to act on what must have often felt to be little more than hazy hunches, despite language such as 'the angel of the Lord said …', or 'the Spirit of the Lord told them …'. Such promptings, and a conviction it was God 'speaking', led Philip, for example, to risk his reputation as a preacher and leave a successful evangelistic and healing ministry in Samaria, to go and stand on the desert road between Jerusalem and Gaza, with no further instructions or explanations (Acts 8:26–40). We find something similar in the following chapter, following Saul's dramatic encounter with the risen Christ on the road to Damascus that left him physically blind. Ananias, whom we haven't heard of before, and doesn't feature by name in Acts again, is told by the Lord in a vision to go and restore the former persecutor's sight. This was not just a risk to his reputation, but, as he expresses it in response to the call, potentially to his life. Nonetheless, out of obedience, he goes; 'attention' has led to 'absorption' and 'action' (Acts 9:10—19).

Some time later, Saul, who by now is known as the Apostle Paul, desperate to preach in the province of Asia, received a vision in the night 'of a man in Macedonia standing and begging him: "Come over to Macedonia and help us." After Paul had seen the vision, we got ready at once to leave for Macedonia, concluding that God had called us to preach the gospel to them' (Acts 16:9–10).

As a result of that 'listening obedience', the church in Philippi was born.

From the very practical New Testament letter of James, it is clear in the first chapter how important he considers listening obedience to be:

Everyone should be quick to listen, slow to speak and slow to become angry ... (Jas. 1:19)

Do not merely listen to the word, and so deceive your-selves. Do what it says. (Jas. 1:22)

WHAT HAPPENS WHEN LEADERS DON'T LISTEN?

Despite the dual command to listen and obey, at times the Old Testament reads like a catalogue of either leaders, or the people of God as a whole, failing to listen, with serious consequences. An illustration of the people being unwilling to listen at the 'absorption' and 'action' levels I have referred to above comes after Moses had finally come to terms with God's call to lead the people out of slavery in Egypt to freedom in the Promised Land. No sooner has the deliverance happened, and they are finally free from the shackles of slavery, than he is beset by problems as a result of their continual complaining and grumbling. It starts almost as soon as the waters of the Red Sea have begun to recede into the distance:

When they came to Marah, they could not drink its water because it was bitter. (That is why the place is called

Marah.) So the people grumbled against Moses saying, 'What are we to drink?' (Ex. 15:23–24)

Despite the miraculous provision they experienced then and subsequently, all of which was evidence of God's love and power, the grumbling continued over the following months and years, as people began to yearn for the 'good old days' back in Egypt. Their failure to listen and obey meant that what should have been a relatively short and straightforward journey to Canaan ended up taking forty years.

To cite another Old Testament example, Saul, having been appointed and anointed as Israel's first king, started well, enjoying successes and God's favour as a result of his obedience. However, as time went on, he became so full of himself, and thereby deaf to God, with the result that the later story of his leadership as King of Israel failed to match up to the earlier expectations and promise. His impulsive nature, jealousy of David, and ultimately his failure to listen and obey, led him to take matters into his own hands, which more and more cut him off from God, as well as alienating him from his own people:

Then the word of the Lord came to Samuel: 'I am grieved that I have made Saul king, because he has turned away from me and has not carried out my instructions.' Samuel was troubled, and he cried out to the Lord all that night. (1 Sam. 15:10–11)

We know too that later King David himself, Saul's successor, the leader described in the New Testament as 'a man after God's own heart', also spectacularly failed in the area of listening obedience. He should have been familiar with Moses' words, as found in Deuteronomy 17:17, that the king 'must not acquire many wives for himself, or else his heart will turn away; also silver and gold he must not acquire in great quantity for himself'.

David heard this (attentiveness), but he failed to listen in terms of absorption and action. Instead he accumulated a considerable number of wives and concubines, including Bathsheba, with whom he committed adultery, and then compounded his disobedience by arranging for her husband Uriah to be killed in battle – an attempt to cover up his sin. A tragic example of a leader not listening, though, as we know through Nathan the prophet's intervention, God spoke to him in such a way that he could later acknowledge his sin and find forgiveness and restoration (Psalm 51 is the expression of this in David's prayer for cleansing and pardon). Despite that early request that God would give him a wise and listening heart, David's son Solomon, who succeeded him as king, again chose not to listen to these same words of Moses, and ended up with 700 princess wives and 300 concubines!

If we fast forward to the seventh and sixth centuries BC, we come across people called into significant leadership roles, like the prophet Jeremiah, who for forty years served as God's spokesperson to the people of Judah. Consistently and passionately he urged the people to listen to God's voice, to turn from their sins and back to God, but it seemed no one was listening. They preferred the softer voices of the false prophets. As a consequence of failing to heed the warnings, Jeremiah was given no choice but to predict the destruction of Jerusalem. That terrible event is described in Chapter 39 of his prophecy, which was followed by decades of exile in Babylon.

Moving once more into the New Testament, the exhortation to listen and the potential consequences of disobedience, are spelled out particularly clearly through the recurring motif of the letters to the Seven Churches, found in Revelation Chapters 2 and 3. The risen Christ says through the Apostle John, at that point in exile on Patmos: 'Whoever has an ear, let them hear what the Spirit says to the churches.' Sadly, it seems that overall there *was* a failure to listen, and heed the warnings that were being given. As a result, with a few notable exceptions, over subsequent centuries, there has been little significant Christian witness or vibrant church presence in the area where those seven churches were located, in what we know as modern day Turkey.

LESSONS FROM 'THEN' TO 'NOW'

The temptation when looking back, whether many centuries to the biblical record, or to more recent Church history, is often to think: 'That was then, this is the twenty-first century; is it therefore appropriate to try and make connections?' Or: '*We* wouldn't make those same mistakes.' But maybe we need to heed what to some might sound like a cliché: 'History repeats itself; it has to, because no one listens.' Thus, to my mind we would be unwise not to heed the warnings of contemporary researchers in the UK, such as Stuart Murray and Peter Brierley. According to Murray's research, for example, if the current rate of decline in church numbers in the United Kingdom continues:

> the Methodist Church will have zero membership by 2037 ... the Church of Scotland will close its last congregation in 2033 ... the Church in Wales will be unsustainable by 2020.[5]

He also reports on the struggles of the Salvation Army in the United Kingdom as well as – again with notable exceptions – consistent decline in church attendance for the Church of England and the Roman Catholic Church in recent decades.

To come at this another way, and offer a specific illustration when it comes to Sundays, we are all aware of how we now live in a 24/7 society, work and leisure patterns having changed radically in the last twenty years. One result is that weekends are understood and lived differently. Furthermore, over this same period we have witnessed a significant increase in the breakdown of family life, with many more single parents or 'blended families' following a first marriage breakdown. This means that children may be with one parent during the week, and another at the weekend.

As I visit parishes in my role as a bishop, I sometimes ask the question: 'Who are your competitors on a Sunday?' Back come answers like: Sunday sport; car boot sales; garden centres; shopping centres; the need to catch up on housework and the garden.

While we may for good reason lament the fact that, for the majority, Sunday is no longer special or different from the rest of the week, and as human beings we neglect the Sabbath principle at our peril, might it not also be the case that we need to move from lament mode to reflection, which in turn leads to fresh and appropriate 'action'. We might recognise as a result that the Spirit is saying that gathering on a 'Sunday-only basis' as the people of God, won't do any more.

WHY LISTENING REMAINS CRUCIAL FOR LEADERS TODAY

In common with leaders in the different eras of the biblical revelation, we may not actually be able to change much of what is going on in society around us. But does that mean we have nothing to say? In fact, 'reading the signs of the times' should offer a challenge to be ahead of the game, rather than always seeming to be responding late in the day, and sometimes too late. I believe that in a context where much is changing and uncertain, listening as a leader is rather like setting a compass. To continue the navigation analogy, we trust that even if the waters are uncharted, and we are not sure what will be encountered *en route*, there is still an overall direction and ultimate destination towards which we can move.

In his book, *Resourcing Renewal,* Martyn Atkins puts it like this:

A crucial part of rapport is genuine listening. Listening to the missionary God, and listening to the world God loves.

For a long time inherited church has operated as if its task was to speak; it was for others to listen. In these post-Christendom times, however, listening, then responding in an authentically Christian way – in chess terms playing black to the world's white move – is better proclamation. Listening enables us to rediscover the gospel as God's good news for our context, and without listening the church can come to hold a gospel that is not encountered as good news. Listening is powerful evangelism today. David Augsburger says, 'Being heard is so close to being loved that for the average person they are almost indistinguishable.' A Spirit-led church that truly listens will change the world.[6]

Many people have written helpfully about some of the major challenges that face leaders in today's Church, especially in what is often described as the post-Christendom west. It is not the purpose of this book to go into detail about these, but it is important to identify some of them, in order that as leaders we can interpret them for ourselves, and those for whom we have responsibility. To repeat the motif from Revelation, we need continually to discern through what is happening 'what the Spirit might be saying to the church' in our own times.

Of the many challenges, in the last part of this chapter I want to identify three in particular that leaders need to heed and respond to, and which can potentially bring fresh hope. The first is *finding ourselves leading from the edge rather than the centre*. This is of course to do with the demise of Christendom, and a Christian faith that once shaped much of society and culture in Western Europe, now no longer doing so. The second is *exercising leadership in a multi-cultural, multi-faith society*. To quote from the title of an excellent book by Andrew Wingate on the subject, what does it mean to be *Celebrating Difference, Staying Faithful*? Thirdly *learning as leaders to ask the right questions in any given situation!*

LEADING FROM THE EDGE

It is clear that the church in the west no longer occupies the centre, or 'high ground'. This can leave church leaders feeling cut off from their 'moorings', and sensing a vulnerability and aloneness in what seems to be an increasingly foreign and antagonistic culture.

However, there are voices that express real hope – not in the reconstitution of Christendom, a going back to some 'good old days', real or imagined – but in the recognition that following the end of this 'modern' era, can come the beginning of a new flowering of Christianity and the Church. One such influential voice is Old Testament scholar, Walter Brueggemann. He identifies many parallels between our contemporary Christian experience of dislocation, irrelevance and uncertainty, and the experience of the Old Testament Jewish exiles in Babylon.[8]

Brueggemann suggests that the experience which faced the Jewish exiles in many ways mirrors the Church's experience today. Some of the parallels he draws are as follows:

- The sense of grieving, loss and struggling with humiliation.
- The ground slipping from under the people of God's feet.
- The sense of lament for what was, and now is not, and will not be again.
- Exiles feeling like a "motherless child" – orphaned, vulnerable, rootless.

He cites material from Lamentations as evidence of the expression of the honest sadness of an exiled people, expressed also in that poignant question from the Psalms:

'How can we sing the Lord's song in a strange land?' (Ps. 137:4)

Reflecting on this, it often seems that when the Church is pushed to the edges there is a danger that leaders need to spot: that of being so preoccupied with survival, its people are unable to step outside themselves and their own concerns to rethink, or re-describe a larger reality. Self-preoccupation does not usually produce energy, courage or freedom! As a result of our own increasingly 'exilic experience' which can produce an unhealthy mixture of fear and nostalgia, the Church and its leaders have too often been focusing on trying to hold on to the plot of ground that is currently being occupied, fearful of losing any more. This means there is then no energy left to re-imagine a robust future for the Church. Again to quote Brueggemann, what exiles must yearn for is an invitation to live: 'freely, dangerously and tenaciously in a world where faith does not have its own way'[9].

For this to happen it needs leaders who learn to discern the 'signs of the times', and thereby to see what hope and possibility there might be for the future. To take an example from Jeremiah 1, the prophet is there given two visions. The first is of an almond tree, and the other of a boiling pot. The almond tree, on that exposed plateau where Jeremiah lived, was always the first tree in spring to show any signs of life after the brutality of winter. It is no accident that we find a play on words going on here, because the Hebrew word for almond comes from the same root as 'to watch'. So in answer to God's question, 'What do you see?', Jeremiah's response could equally be: 'I see the branch of an almond tree or a "watching" tree' (Jer. 1:11–12) It is as if God were saying: 'Yes there is exile and judgment to be faced – the later vision of the boiling pot makes that clear (1:13–16) – a lot of uncertainty lies ahead, but I, God, am at work; I am watching what is going on, and I need *you* to be watching too'.

Reading the signs of the time, and becoming bearers of hope, seem to me to be essential qualities to be developed in those who lead 'from the edge' – a hope that could be defined as being in a costly yet real relationship with what is going on around, neither 'head in the sand' nor filled with gloom and despair. In partnership with others, it is vital to be readers of and listeners to what is influencing culture, globally, nationally and locally. This is often not an easy or comfortable place for a leader to be, but further evidence as to why it will involve considerable 'listening skills' at many different levels. When we pause to reflect, is there not much evidence throughout history that the renewal of the church often comes from the edges?

LISTENING LEADERS IN A MULTI-FAITH SOCIETY

Again, it is not within the scope of this book to go into detail in this area, but we are all affected by the changed nature of UK society as we experience it in the early years of the twenty-first century. This is true whether we live and work in an area of significant ethnic diversity or not. We are all part of what is often described as a 'post 9–11, post 7–7 world', and are all affected by what has come to be known as globalisation.

Globalisation is certainly an economic phenomenon, but it also affects communication, terrorism and security measures and sport, as well as cultural and religious trends. As Malcolm Duncan has expressed it:

> Globalisation is not just about what is exported "from the West to the rest". It is a highway upon which ideologies, religions, spiritualities and world views travel at breakneck speed.[10]

What this means in practice is that the people who make up our communities bring with them potentially colliding world-views and ideas that we would not have been exposed to, even thirty years ago.

Where multi-culturalism and religious pluralism were once unusual phenomena, this is no longer the case in an increasingly interconnected and mobile world. In the 2001 UK Census, 40 million people described their religion as 'Christian' (almost 70% of the population).

However, those who made up the remaining 30% reveal the extent of the diversity of religious and cultural life in this country. Christianity has over recent decades been joined in the UK by the 'traditional' religions of Judaism, Islam, Hinduism, Buddhism and Sikhism, as well as other newer expressions of spirituality. Each religious group or community has developed in a different way, as a result of the diversity of its origins and the distinctives – ethnic, religious, cultural and economic – of both the groups in question and the host community.

Despite all the evidence around us of these developments, for some, it seems, there is an attempt to pretend that really, nothing has changed. Even more sadly, we sometimes witness churches and their members, in more or less subtle ways, colluding with some of the ill-informed prejudices evident in society. In the light of this, it can be quite a task for the Christian leader not only to hear for themselves, but also to be an interpreter of what God might be saying through this changed and changing situation.

To take one example, how many people are aware that the United Kingdom has the fifth largest Jewish community in the world after the United States, Israel, the former Soviet Union and France? Their numbers are not as great as they were in the 1950s, but for churches and their leaders in certain parts of cities such as Manchester, Leeds, Glasgow and London, a commitment to listening needs to involve understanding of, and, where possible, relationship and dialogue with, those who also look to Abraham as their spiritual father.

Having lived and worked in several northern towns and cities where there are significant numbers of people from different ethnic and religious backgrounds, I am well aware that broad generalisations as to how people understand and express their faith are unlikely to be helpful; they usually do more harm than good!

To illustrate from the British Muslim community, it is important that leaders help people to understand that the Muslim community is not homogenous in background, attitude or outlook. Muslim attitudes towards Muslim schools are, for example, divided. Similarly there are differing opinions on whether their women should wear the *niqab* – the complete physical covering.

At the time of 9–11, when I was living and working in Bradford, a small minority of the many mosques in the City were supportive of Osama bin Laden and Al Qaeda. But the vast majority of Muslims were as horrified as everyone else by the 2001 terrorist attack on the Twin Towers. We recognise that here may be a small but significant minority in our communities influenced by radicalisation, but this is of as much concern to many of the Muslim community leaders as it is for the rest of the population.

The so-called 'Bradford riots' of 2001 in fact give a positive example of the importance of the Church and its leaders listening, in a situation where there was tension and suspicion. Much damage was done in the Manningham area of the city as a result of a number of disaffected young men from the Asian community going on the rampage. Two things in particular emerged from this. One was an acknowledgement, on behalf of many of the 'elders' of the Muslim community, that some of their young people were 'out of control' – an admission of need, effectively asking for help from the wider community. The other concerned a group of church leaders who, the day after the riots, walked through the streets of the affected area, praying and giving out written messages of love and reconciliation on behalf of the Christian community. There were people from the Muslim community weeping in the streets at this response from Christians. A 'theatre of prayer' was also set up in one of the Anglican churches in the area, to which people of all faiths and none were invited. Out of a situation of crisis, here was a powerful example of 'listening obedience' on the part of leaders from many different Christian communities.

I am well aware that there have always been different viewpoints as to how Christians should relate to people of other faiths. In essence there seem to be four 'options', and even saying this I am conscious of the limitations of language and understanding. The first is *separation*, where local churches and their leaders choose not to work with anyone from a different faith, for fear of compromise. The second approach might be called *assimilation*. Here, Christians and expressions of local church seem to be content that their ethos or work does not need to be distinctive. The *multi-faith* approach has often been seen as affirming all the various expressions of faith as coming from, and ultimately leading back to, the same source. In the *inter-faith* approach, which is the one increasingly found to be helpful and appropriate, distinctives between faiths are acknowledged and affirmed, with dialogue recognised as the best way forward, and a commitment to working together where there is common ground and areas of common concern. Here, *listening* and *discussion* are essential tools and people are able to celebrate their distinctives, leading to greater understanding, which in turn leads to a promotion of better social harmony. (I will return to this again in the chapter on 'Learning to listen to those from whom we differ').

In all this, acknowledging that there will be different perspectives, it seems to me that if Christ were walking the streets of our towns and cities today, among people of different ethnicities, whatever else he might do, he would be listening, and wanting to build relationships. He would be offering the hospitality of time and attentiveness. He who was 'grace and truth' embodied (John 1:14), surely looks for that same combination to be found in his Church. Through listening, we are able to see where there is common ground, and equally where we might need to agree to differ, or, in a right spirit, challenge – but listening has to come first.

THE LEADER'S ROLE IN ASKING QUESTIONS

In the unchartered waters in which the Church finds itself, the third key responsibility of the listening leader is to be one who asks questions – of God, the Church and the wider community – and then listens to and seeks to discern the significance of what is coming back from or out of those different sources.

If we need it, there is much good biblical precedent for asking God questions! Whether these come from the mouths of a reluctant Jonah, and his trying to fathom out what God's purposes are for the people of Nineveh, or, in the New Testament, the wrestling that had to go on at the Council of Jerusalem as the Jewish mother church tried to come to terms with the Gentile believers having an equal share in God's salvation (see Acts 15), leaders have key roles in asking questions.

Furthermore, much of Jesus' ministry consisted of asking questions. Indeed, the evidence of the New Testament is that he asked more questions than he gave answers!

Thus, at a key point in his ministry, after the Transfiguration, at Caesarea Philippi he asked his disciples: 'Who do you say that I am?' (Luke 9:20).

To the religious leaders, amazed at the healing of the paralysed man, and yet appalled at his claim to forgive sins, he asked: 'Why are you thinking these things? Which is easier: to say to the paralytic, "Your sins are forgiven", or to say, "Get up, take your mat and walk"?' (Mark 2:9).

At the end of many of his parables, he would ask a question such as: 'Which of these three do you think was a neighbour to the man who fell into the hands of robbers?' (Luke 10:36).

Those called into leadership need to be asking questions, not only in the areas of doctrine and belief, crucial as these are, but also in terms of the Church's priorities. At the broader canvas level this might be in relation to a diocese, district or province. They may be 'big picture' questions concerned with overall strategy, vision, values and goals. How is the diocese/district/province seeking to discern the priorities God wants to see fulfilled?

At local level they might be much more basic questions such as: 'Why are we continuing with this piece of work or organisation, when it is sapping the energy of those involved, and clearly past its "sell-by date"?' 'Given that we can't do everything, what is that as a church or churches together we can distinctively contribute to the wider life of the community where we are placed, that no-one else is doing?' 'Which groups of people that live in our parish or area are under-represented in our church community, and how might that change?' 'Why, if people these days are searching spiritually, is the Church often the last place they look for answers?' 'On a scale of 1 to 10, how concerned are current church members for the well-being and coming to faith of those who are not yet Christians?' 'What will best enable those who are already Christians to grow in their faith and live out a "whole-life discipleship"?'

Having identified what questions might need to be asked, it is then vital to have a process by which listening and reflection can take place, and possible steps forward identified. I will develop this further in the chapter on 'Creating a listening church', but for now it is impossible to overstate the leader's key role in making it a priority to 'listen to what the Spirit is saying to the church', not least through the circumstances of our world, the Church and the lives of individuals.

Chapter two

Barriers and obstacles for leaders learning to listen

Just before the outbreak of the Second World War, German theologian Dietrich Bonhoeffer wrote his seminal book *Life Together,* drawing on his experience of training future leaders in a theological seminary. In it, he observed:

> Christians have forgotten that the ministry of listening has been committed to them by him who is himself the great listener and whose work they should share. We should listen with ears of God that we may speak the word of God.[1]

Those of us in leadership roles know the truth of this in theory, but for many of us there seem to be obstacles and barriers that get in the way of that quality of listening. We seem to live with the illusion that speaking, whether to God or others, is more important than listening. Some of the obstacles set out below are common to anyone trying to make sense of life in the twenty-first century, but I believe they affect leaders in a particular way.

BUSYNESS

Where shall the word be found, where will the word resound?

Not here, there is not enough silence ...

So wrote T. S. Eliot in his 1930 poem 'Ash Wednesday'[2]. Further on in the poem, he says: 'Against the Word the unstilled world still whirled' – a powerful way of expressing how in our busy and often restless lives, there seems to be too little time to reflect or think. 'Only the wind will listen'.

Like me, you may have been challenged – not to mention made to feel guilty! – by phrases like 'the barrenness of a busy life', or 'the urgent crowding out the important'. In one sense, there is nothing new about busyness when it comes to ministry and leadership, and 'busy' in itself isn't necessarily bad. As Michael Mitton has expressed it: 'What is wrong is where there is no freedom to pause, and also where there is activity without receptivity.'[3]

The Gospels, for example, don't give a picture of Jesus spending his time waiting by lakesides or sitting on top of mountains wondering how to fill his day. It is clear that on a daily basis he felt the pressure of people's demands on him and those he had called to be with him. (In the later chapter, 'Silence for the leader – friend or foe?', I will focus on the way in which, in the first six chapters of Mark's Gospel, we see Jesus balancing intense activity among people with intentional time alone with his Father, at the heart of which was stillness and listening.) However, ministry is exercised in a particular time context, and there are certain factors about life in the twenty-first century that cause busyness to be a particular issue.

It was in 1980 that *TIME* magazine predicted that, with all the fast-moving developments in technology, by the turn of the new millennium in 2000 most people in the western world would only be working three or four days a week, and would therefore have to find new ways to fill all their increased leisure time! While this may have come true for a minority, for the rest of us a response of hollow laughter is more likely, as we find ourselves caught up not just in busy lives, but ones which are as a result often stress-filled and, as one American writer has put it, 'hurry-sick'. In the United Kingdom, as in much of the rest of the western world, this is largely rooted in the way life changed in the 1980s, when the market economy and consumerist lifestyle began to dominate and shape our lives. We all continue to reap the consequences, whether or not we actually ever embraced its philosophy.

In addition to being caught up in this like everyone else, for leaders in most of the mainstream denominations there are three other factors that seem to compound the increased busyness. The first is that with many church members' lives being so full with work and family commitments, they have little time and energy left with which to offer their gifts and service in and through the body of Christ. Responsible leaders are reluctant to add further burdens. This in turn means even more pressure being placed on the few who do have time and space. Add to this – with notable exceptions – significant numerical decline in most mainstream denominations over the last thirty years, and the few (who are also often older) volunteers become fewer still. Thirdly, with the fall in vocations to full-time stipendiary ministry in most denominations, and large numbers retiring not matched by those beginning ministry, many clergy not only in rural, but now also in urban areas, have to take responsibility for several congregations. It is not surprising that, unless new ways of exercising and expressing leadership are developed, this kind of busyness, as well as sapping morale, may lead to burnout, if not complete breakdown.

It is therefore not surprising, in the light of these and other factors, that making space and time for listening to God, which has never been easy to keep as a priority, ends up getting completely squeezed out. As one parish priest said to me:

> Apart from the sheer lack of time, it can feel self-indulgent or just plain selfish to set time aside for this, when there is so much to be done. Anyway, the rest of my congregation don't have that luxury, so why should I?

Many reading this book will, I feel sure, readily identify with his honesty. Yet, without recognition of the importance of the practice of listening, and the willingness to march to a different drumbeat, barrenness and exhaustion rather than fruitfulness and fulfilment are likely to be the outcome. A struggle for some in this area, especially those of a more activist disposition, might be because they see the opposite of busyness as passivity. I would suggest that this is a misapprehension of what it means to 'wait on God', which in the Scriptures is always to be understood as something active, holding a sense of anticipation; for example, Psalm 27:14: 'Wait for the Lord; be strong and take heart and wait for the Lord', or Jesus' command to the disciples in Luke 24:49: 'Wait in the city until you have been clothed with power from on high'.

Over-busyness also diminishes our capacity to 'see', in the sense of being truly attentive and fully present to what is around us. In the play *St Joan*, by George Bernard Shaw, one of the characters asks Joan of Arc why the voice of God never speaks to him as she claims it constantly speaks to her. 'The voice speaks to you all the time', she says. 'You fail to listen.'

To quote a C. S. Lewis phrase, 'God may be affecting our consciousness', but we are not 'aware' that this thought or insight is coming from God. Thus we can miss the burning bush that might be right in front of us, as expressed in the memorable words of Elizabeth Barrett-Browning's sonnet:

> Earth's crammed with heaven
> And every common bush afire with God.
> But only he who sees takes off his shoes,
> The rest sit round and pluck blackberries.

Or, like Eli in 1 Samuel 3, we fail to be alert as quickly as we might to the significance of the voice speaking in the night – the sometimes ordinary and at other times surprising ways God may want to speak to us.

A renewed understanding, drawing on the Celtic tradition, is proving helpful for some in addressing the contemporary challenges we face. The Celts believed that they could encounter God anywhere, even in the midst of the ordinariness and busyness of daily life. Unlike our modernist western mindset, they did not compartmentalise the 'sacred' and the 'secular', the 'spiritual' and the 'natural'. Seeing God's creation as a sacrament enabled a sense of expectancy and alertness that some today are rediscovering, not least through the disciplines of what is sometimes called 'the new monasticism'. Books by David Adam, formerly based on Lindisfarne, liturgies emerging from places like the Community of Aidan and Hilda, also on Lindisfarne, or the mainland-based Northumbria Community's 'Celtic Daily Prayer', offer a fresh sense of rhythm and a greater capacity to be aware of 'God in everything' to many Christians, lay and ordained.

I am an activist by nature, with a ministry as a Bishop which, while it is an enormous privilege, is also demanding and, if I allow it to be, can be all-consuming. In my experience, it can take courage to stop and make time to be still, to listen and to wait on God. It seems as though while complaining about our busyness we might sometimes be afraid, wondering what will happen to our work, to ourselves and others' expectations, if we dare to stop, look and listen.

TIREDNESS

A close cousin of over-busyness, not surprisingly, is over-tiredness. Back in the 1980s, through his research on clergy stress, John Sandford identified 'the job is never finished' as being one of the main causes of clergy burnout.[4] Nearly thirty years on, research has revealed that in the United Kingdom, not only are many people working longer hours than they used to but we are sleeping on average two hours a night less. Responding to the advice from some that sleeping for one hour less a night could add three years to our lives, so we can fit more in, is hardly helpful! As well as its other side effects, there is no doubt that over-tiredness saps our capacity to concentrate and, thereby, to listen.

In his book, *The Busy Christian's Guide to Busyness,* Tim Chester writes:

'Here's the deal: God made human beings and he built in a need to sleep. People who think they can operate with little sleep are defying God's created order ... God didn't make you to miss sleep. Sleeping is not unrighteous. God gave us sleep as a gift.'[5]

The problem is that some of us as leaders think of ourselves as Superman or Superwoman, and this means somehow we are magically or supernaturally protected from the impact that over-tiredness and lack of sleep can bring to others. If this is the case, we should perhaps turn our attention again to the words of Psalm 127:2: 'In vain you rise up early and stay up late, toiling for food to eat – for he grants sleep to those he loves.'

Staying with the Old Testament, the experience of the prophet Elijah – a key leader in his time – gives us one of the classic biblical examples of the effects of over-tiredness. Following the famous victory at Mount Carmel over the prophets of Baal, he is on the run from Queen Jezebel, and finally falls exhausted: '"I have had enough Lord", he said. "Take my life; I am no better than my ancestors." Then he lay down under the tree and fell asleep' (1 Kings 19:4–5).

How wonderful that, following his admission of the effects of pressure and exhaustion, God's response was neither one of rebuke, nor that he should get up earlier the next day to pray in order to be in a better spiritual frame of mind! Rather it was to refresh Elijah with sleep, and when he woke up to provide him with a good meal. Furthermore, out of this 'enforced stop', having rested and then moved on at a slower pace, he was then at a place to 'hear' God when he spoke, not this time through the earthquake, wind and fire, but in a *gentle whisper*' (1 Kings 19:12). It is healthier to make the choice to stop and listen, because if we don't, we may reap serious consequences.

THE DIFFICULTY OF STOPPING

I have had the privilege of having the same spiritual director for almost thirty years, and am more grateful than I can express in words for the challenges and insights he has offered me, not least in this area of learning to listen to God. But I well remember, with some discomfort, the first time I went to meet him at the Community of the Resurrection at Mirfield. I was a year or so into my first incumbency, in a challenging urban parish in West Yorkshire. We were seeing many encouragements, signs of life and growth in the church, but I was working in such a way that I knew meant I couldn't keep up the pace I had set myself, with little or no time for reflection, nor, to be honest as I look back, sufficient quality time for my family. So I approached my first meeting with a mixture of both anxiety and anticipation.

The first words that came from him were ones of apology: something urgent had cropped up that he had to deal with, so would I mind sitting and waiting in one of the guest rooms for half an hour. I replied that I would actually be pleased to enjoy a little uninterrupted space. For the first few moments all was well, but as time went on, I had that experience which Henri Nouwen describes so graphically of my mind being 'like a banana tree, filled with monkeys constantly jumping up and down. A mind rarely still and quiet.'

Imagine my consternation when my Spiritual Director reappeared, folded his hands on his lap, and without any preamble asked, 'So what has Jesus been saying to you over this last half hour?' I can't now remember what my reply was, but it very clearly revealed to me an ambivalence: a longing in the midst of busyness to be able to stop and listen, and yet when the opportunity was there, not quite knowing how to handle it, because there was so much 'stuff' going on inside. Or, to express it another way, part of us wants to 'hear from God', but another part worries that in so doing our lifestyle, attitudes and priorities might be seriously challenged. I know others in leadership, especially those like me of a more activist disposition, who would identify with this.

Much of this is the difficulty of being 'in the present'. Children have a particular ability to be completely present to the moment, unaware of time, lost in whatever it is they are engaged in. I still have memories from my childhood of playing in or around the garden shed in our Vicarage garden, being vaguely conscious of a voice in the distance telling me that lunch was ready. When I finally arrived in the kitchen, my mum would say, not in a scolding tone but nonetheless clearly surprised: 'Didn't you know what the time was?'

I came to realise a few years ago that (with the combination of my particular personality and increased leadership responsibilities) I had largely lost this capacity of 'being in the present'. I was more conscious, to quote the *Anglican Book of Common Prayer*, of 'the things I had done or left undone', or of what was to be done next, than what J. P. de Cassaude refers to as 'the sacrament of the present moment'.

We know in our heads that this present moment is all we can be certain we have (and some of us have probably preached eloquent sermons on the subject to others!) but when it comes to the present, we are *not* present, either with ourselves, God or other people. Again, it seems that one of the consequences of the pace and style of twenty-first century life leads us to see time only in chronological terms – a finite supply of minutes, hours, days, weeks and years. We have lost an understanding of '*kairos*' – discerning the significance of eternity within a given single moment. Was this not something of what Jesus encouraged the three disciples to grasp, on the Mount of Transfiguration? Here, Peter, James and John were invited to step aside from the busyness of life and ministry with Jesus and, while there with him on the mountain, heard the invitation to listen, in effect, to be present to the voice that came from the cloud.

Fear can also be a more powerful force than we realise in contributing to our difficulties in being willing to 'be still and know that I am God' (Ps. 46:10). This can manifest itself in a number of ways. There is the fear of being alone with ourselves or God. Linked to this is the fear of intimacy. Bill Hybels, the Founding and Senior Pastor of Willow Creek Community Church in Chicago, expressed it this way at a leadership conference I attended: 'Leaders need to be aware that doing God's work can destroy the work of God in us.'

Ironically, when relationship is at the heart of Christian faith and ministry, our work calling can become a means of avoiding closeness with other people and with God. Also, because it is difficult to measure the 'results' of our ministry, we can be afraid of stopping, in case, by doing so, we somehow will have to face what we perceive to be areas of failure and disappointment in our lives and ministries. The result can be that we work harder and faster to try and compensate.

A further factor that can contribute to the difficulty of stopping and listening is an over-inflated view of our own indispensability as leaders. Few of us could justify this theologically, nor would we want to admit to it too publicly, but our lifestyles and diaries, in whatever way we keep them, suggest otherwise. We know in theory it is an arrogant, ego-centric position to take up. 'Unless the Lord builds the house we labour in vain' (Ps. 127:1–3).

We know that Christ said *he* would build his church (Matt. 16:18), but somehow we live and work in a way that suggests it all depends on *us*. That in turn can also collude with the expectations that some congregation members have of their leaders – always available; never off duty. It seems some of us have seriously misinterpreted the words recorded in John 5:16, where Jesus said 'My Father is always working, and I am always working'!

Another barrier to leaders being willing to stop and listen is actually to do with the issue of control. We are not in control when we are truly listening – in whatever way and whether directly to God, or to another human being – as we are when we are speaking. Listen to Bonhoeffer's wisdom again:

> Christians, especially ministers, so often think they must always contribute something when they are in the company of others, that this is the one service they can render.[6]

We think we always have to be problem-solvers, coming up with solutions for everyone's needs and issues, able to bring words of comfort for every person in pain, whereas in fact what many people need is simply to be listened to. If we as leaders are not intentional about listening to God, nor making space for ourselves, we are unlikely to be of much help to others.

Stopping and listening also means being open to change, which can be costly, so again we find that ambivalence of being drawn and yet fearful at the same time.

In his helpful book *Do Nothing to Change Your Life*, Bishop Stephen Cottrell speaks of a need for human beings to be 'eccentric'. Some might say clergy, of all people, need no encouragement to be eccentric, but he is referring to a true understanding of the word – i.e. losing the need to be the centre of the universe. He recognises that this is very counter-cultural, challenging the right to self-fulfilment, a high value in today's world. But stillness, and thereby learning to listen, is, he says, to repeat the earlier analogy, like resetting the compass of our lives:

> To put God at the centre is not to fill a gap. It is much more like resetting a compass. It is with God, and the knowledge of God at the centre of your life, that the joy and meaning and purpose that you have already found within yourself, can be redirected and multiplied, bringing greater joy and greater peace.[7]

TECHNOLOGY – A BARRIER AS WELL AS BLESSING

As I expressed it earlier, ministry always takes place in context, and even though *TIME* magazine's predictions about life and leisure were seriously flawed, and the 'paperless office' continues to be a myth, most of us now take for granted at least some of the benefits of technology such as the Internet and communication by e-mail. So many aspects of communication are immediate, faster and more efficient than ever before. But there are also downsides to these developments. Until the last few years, for example, letters were dated by day, whereas e-mails can be clocked not just to the minute, but the second, and thereby in some people's minds demand an instant response. In our mobile phone culture, through which we can now also access our e-mails, the expectation from others or ourselves that we are always available seems to be increased. As long ago now as the turn of the millennium, Richard Powers wrote about the 'contagion of real time':

> In real time, every second counts. Every minute must be maximised. Since we cannot stop the escaping moments, we have our machines give us the next best thing: two moments crammed into one. Split screen. Multitasking. Mobile wireless voicemail message forwarding. RSS feeds. Picture-in-a-picture. We don't need to miss a thing. In fact, we can't ... in real time, we live in two minds, three tenses and four continents at once ... In short we have grown so used to mastering time that nanoseconds weigh heavy on our hands.[8]

According to the same author, the number of people who always felt rushed in their working lives jumped 50% between the 1960s and 1990s.

This expectation of immediate response, and consequent sense of rush and pressure, can also have the effect of diminishing our capacity or availability to encounter God. What do I mean by this? For some in leadership – as with the rest of humankind! – along with what comes in our direction over which we may not have control, there is the temptation to spend so much time in front of the PC or laptop: 'Just another few minutes while I check my e-mails/research this on the net/prepare my power point!' The result? Another opportunity to make time to listen for the still small voice, or be with people and their needs, is squeezed out. If we are not careful, there is something addictive or seductive about technology, with the result that, as in other areas of life, the good becomes the enemy of the best.

To give a specific illustration of these dangers, I was once on a retreat with some other clergy, which began on a Monday evening. The silence was due to begin during the course of Tuesday morning, so at breakfast there was the usual kind of conversation about how well or otherwise people had slept. One minister, who was last down, looked as though he had experienced a poor night, and on being asked how his sleep had been, replied: 'I had a terrible night. I shouldn't have done it, but I decided to check my e-mails before I went to bed, and there was a particularly nasty one from someone in the congregation. I wish I hadn't bothered, but the problem is, you get into the habit of doing it last thing at night and it's hard to break.'

Even though he had set aside time for an individually-guided retreat, recognising the importance of it to help him learn to hear 'the sounds of God better', he had been caught out by the addictive nature of technology. It took him a further twenty-four hours to recover any sense of peace, and find some distance from the demands of day-to-day ministry. I hasten to say I don't quote this to stand in judgment of a fellow minister, but because I too have made that same kind of mistake, and paid the price!

Even that old-fashioned instrument the landline telephone can be a barrier to a healthy rhythm of life and ministry. I have had more than one conversation with a priest friend of mine, who regularly answers the phone during meal times, despite the fact that she has an answer phone. In so many different ways in today's world we find ourselves caught up in this expectation of immediate response, even when in any case that may not be the best. We are robbed of time to reflect, and I know a number of leaders who when it comes to e-mails regret pressing the 'send' button, and say they would have responded differently to a situation, had they taken more time to think, pray and listen first.

IS GOD STILL SPEAKING TODAY?

A question for some is around another kind of ambivalence, or perhaps uncertainty, as to whether God is still in the business of 'speaking' today. In the film *The Search for Signs of Intelligent Life in the Universe*, the actress Lily Tomlin's character has a fascinating line:

> Why is it that when we speak to God we are said to be praying, but when God speaks to us we are said to be schizophrenic?

In the New Testament, as has already been noted briefly, the writer to the Hebrews speaks of a God who 'speaks at many times and in various ways', looking back in that context to what we now know as the Old Testament (Heb. 1:1). He then goes on to reflect on the way in which 'in these last days he has spoken to us by his Son, whom he appointed heir of all things, and through whom he made the universe' (Heb. 1:2). For me here, the key words are 'many' and 'various', with Scripture being the touchstone against which we test the validity of what is 'spoken'. This and other biblical passages, not least in some of St Paul's letters, suggest we should have an expectation that God will continue to speak, as a result of the restored relationship made possible through the incarnation, life, death, resurrection and ascension of Christ, and through the gifts and ongoing ministry of the Holy Spirit. Because relationship is at the heart of Christian faith, by definition this involves communication, and communication is a two-way process, again experienced in a variety of ways.

If we limit ourselves by operating only at the cerebral or rational level, then this can sometimes be a barrier. The place of intuition is also important. Anyone who is familiar with the Myers-Briggs Personality Type Indicator process, or other similar resources, will be aware that some people are by nature more intuitive than others, in the way they process and respond to information. This is all to do with that part of the brain which handles emotion, is creative, which dreams and maybe 'sees' pictures. Whether or not we are by nature intuitive, it is important that as leaders we explore what, again to use Myers-Briggs language, might be called the 'shadow' side of our personalities. Sadly, especially in western Protestantism, the area of the intuitive has sometimes been closed off, or people are suspicious of it.

Over thirty years ago, Christopher Bryant wrote this:

Faith has been called a kind of knowledge, an intuitive awareness of the unseen. Intuition has been described as the perception by way of the unconscious. To know by intuition is to know without being able to say how you know. This quality of faith adds conviction to bare belief. 'Faith makes us certain of realities we do not see' (Heb. 11:1).[9]

Caricatures as to how God may or may not speak can be a further significant obstacle, sometimes leading to cynicism. For example, giving an impression that it is possible for leaders to access some kind of 'inside information' or 'hotline' to God, putting one person at an advantage over another, is clearly untrue theologically, as well as potentially doing untold damage to an individual or congregation. Sadly, there are many examples from the past and present where leaders have suggested they have this kind of power, and people have been manipulated and deeply hurt as a result. When leaders use spiritual language, such as 'the Lord has told me ...', as a pre-emptive strike to discourage criticisms of changes being proposed, or as a way of steamrollering a decision, for example about re-ordering a church building, I believe this amounts to nothing less than spiritual abuse.

Equally, I know leaders who have been on the receiving end of so-called 'prophetic' messages from their congregations that have seriously undermined their ministry. Apart from the hurt and damage caused by such attitudes and actions, which often betray power-seeking, not surprisingly it can make leaders closed to the possibility of God speaking in more intuitive ways in the future. As always, the answer to abuse is not non-use, but to put caution and appropriate tests in place, so that what is authentic can be rightly discerned.

For leaders, 'familiarity' with the things of God, leading to cynicism, or what the Bible sometimes refers to as 'hardness of heart', can also be an obstacle to hearing from Him. Sometimes this comes about as a result of earlier disappointments caused by God seeming to be silent, when we have been desperate to hear from him. It is certainly one of the commonest reasons in the Old Testament for leaders, and the people of God in general, failing to hear God's voice. A classic example is found in Psalm 95, words said by many Anglican clergy in the course of Morning Prayer:

> For he is our God, and we are the people of his pasture, the flock under his care. Today if you hear his voice, *do not harden your hearts* as you did at Meribah, as you did at that day at Massah in the desert. (Ps. 95:7–8)

In the New Testament, a phrase that is frequently on Jesus' lips, especially directed at the twelve disciples, to whom he will entrust the future ministry of the Church, is: 'Whoever has ears let them hear' (e.g. Matt. 13:9).

The problem can be that as leaders, over time, we become so focused on the role and responsibilities entrusted to us, we cease to expect that God might actually want to communicate with us. Roy Oswald's experience as a church leader may well find an echo from us:

Pastors face unique problems, I believe, in keeping fresh spiritually. For one thing, the spiritual disciplines we learned as children and young adults are now the tools of our trade. For me, Scripture, prayer and worship became over familiar, and lost much of their mystery. It was difficult to read the Bible devotionally when I knew I had to prepare a sermon from those texts. I felt so much pressure to come up with something meaningful to say that I read the Bible as though I were on a scavenger hunt! *Everything I read was directed to others' needs and not my own* (italics mine) ... I failed to recognise the essential difference between nurturing the spiritual journey of another and having a unique spiritual journey of my own.[10]

Another challenge to the expectation that God will speak into a situation today, is that somehow this is a way for leaders of avoiding risks, offering some kind of insurance policy against failure. After all are we not called to 'walk by faith, not by sight'? In fact, if we study leaders in the biblical revelation, significant leaders down the course of Christian history, or people we know personally who have been most effective, we will find that they are usually risk-takers. They step out in faith, in one way or another, with no assurance of what the outcome will be. From Abram and his response to God's call to leave 'country, people and household' (Gen. 12:1), through to Peter's courage in responding to God speaking through the strange rooftop vision (Acts 10:9ff), and beyond, we see faith is indeed spelled R-I-S-K. When it comes to Paul's response to the vision of a man from Macedonia, since this represented a complete change of plan, it would have been easy for him to dismiss this as being down to an overactive imagination. But as we have already noted, his risk-taking led, albeit at some cost, to the establishing of a new church in Philippi (Acts 16:11ff).

Just over two centuries later, when he was in church one day, and the reading was from Acts 4, describing the first Christian community and its shared life and values, a young man called Antony acted on what he had 'heard', giving away land and selling possessions. This in turn led him to spend many years in solitude, listening for the voice of God. He emerged from this solitude as a healer, teacher and spiritual master, who encouraged others to take up solitary desert life, and became an inspiration to many down the centuries in daring to live a radical life of listening and generosity.

We will all have our own examples of those for whom listening to God meant risk-taking. A deliberately eclectic selection of mine would include not only well-known figures from Church life and history, like St Francis of Assisi, Julian of Norwich, John Wesley, Dietrich Bonhoeffer, Brother Roger of *Taizé*, Archbishops Janani Luwum and Oscar Romero, Mother Teresa and David Watson, but also my training incumbent when I was a curate – Tom Anscombe.

Anyone assuming leadership responsibilities knows that decision-making can be a lonely business, and for some of us even small decisions can cause considerable anxiety. But I hope the examples I have given above, and many others that could be cited, make it clear that the notion of God guiding and speaking is not a short-cut to escape making those crucial decisions or taking risks. Part of the route to further maturity for the leader is navigating the choices and risks in such a way that we begin to develop better judgment and clearer discernment. We will not learn this solely by thinking, reading or studying, but also by acting, taking risks and engaging out on the 'field of play'.

BACK TO BENEDICT!

Later chapters will develop in more detail some of the areas in which we are called to listen, but I end this chapter focusing as it has been on some of the barriers to listening, with reference to the injunction with which the *Holy Rule* of St Benedict opens. It is very simply the word *'Listen'*. Monastic life is a way of life devoted to the practised art of listening. And to any who might think it is easier for a monk or nun to 'hear' God than for the rest of us, because of their particular call, I would urge you to speak to a member of a religious order! I guarantee they would give you a different story. This is why Benedict says: 'Listen carefully, my son, to the master's instructions, and attend to them with the ear of your heart'. In the immediate context in which he is speaking, Benedict is referring to the words of the Lord as they are expressed in the *Rule*, and for the benefit of and ministry of a particular community. But through the centuries, monks and others have learned from that listening, that the scope of things to which they listen, and through which God can speak, grows ever wider. Benedict and others, like the Celts who followed on, teach us that we can listen for the sounds of God anywhere and everywhere – there is nowhere God is not, and no one or no means by which he cannot speak. Once that barrier is recognised, and down, more listening is bound to be possible.

Chapter three

Silence for the leader – friend or foe?

Silence is the language God speaks, and everything else is a bad translation. (Thomas Keating)[1]

Holy Saturday seems to me to describe the place in which many of us live our lives: waiting for God to speak. (Pete Greig)[2]

The experience of God's silence, or even his absence, is not uncommon in the Christian life, especially among those whom God uses most powerfully. (Pete Greig)[3]

In the SOMA (Sharing of Ministries Abroad) course for leaders and church members, 'Listening to God's Voice' (SOMA 1997), which was originally written for a local church, the author and former Director of SOMA, Don Brewin, has this to say:

Silence is not the exclusive prerogative of monasteries, convents or desert places; it is not necessarily a place but a state of heart and mind. It can be found in the midst of ordinary, everyday activities. It may be a small solitude, a little desert, a tiny pool of silence made holy by God's presence there. When we are attuned to God, then He can in the middle of the busyness and rush of life say: 'I will lead you into solitude, and there I shall speak to your heart' (Hos. 2:14). God calls us to stand still before him and listen –while we continue to walk with those around.

I imagine most of us reading these words would find it hard to disagree with the sentiments expressed. But from my own experience as well as observation of others in leadership, the very word 'silence' can cause an ambivalence in us: on the one hand it draws us as something we long for and know we need, and yet, as we have already noted, we continue to fail to make it a priority in the busyness of our lives.

In the light of such ambivalence, I want to explore the absolute necessity of the place of silence as gift for an effective ministry, but also to recognise that there can be another kind of silence, which feels more like the absence of God. This can be difficult enough in itself and for ourselves, but doubly so when, as leaders, we are supposed to be those who have a role to 'hear' God for others and for the church. In this sense silence can appear to be both friend and foe!

THE BENEFITS OF SILENCE IN A HURRY-SICK WORLD

Silence is a key strand of Christian spirituality, not least because it is intended to enable our minds and imaginations to focus and centre on God's living presence, as well as often being the necessary precursor for hearing God. Indeed, one of the most important movements in Eastern Christianity takes its name from the Greek term for 'silence' or 'stillness' – *hesychia* – a word that encompasses both inward and outward silence. This is well illustrated in these words from a former Archbishop of Canterbury:

> Silence enables us to be aware of God, to let mind and imagination dwell upon his truth, to let prayer be listening before it is talking, and to discover our own selves in a way that it is not possible when we are making or listening to noise. (Michael Ramsey)[4]

Silence can also set us free from preoccupation with ourselves and our ministry concerns, as in the presence of God we discover a fresh perspective on who he is, as well as on the situations that concern us.

Our present day society tends to be stress-filled and what James Gleick (in his book *Faster: The Acceleration of Just About Everything*) calls 'hurry-sick'. It is therefore a hard but important lesson to learn, to 'waste time with God'.

From a very different, earlier era, the Venerable Bede said of King Edwin that he was a wise and prudent man, as a result of often taking time to sit in silence for long periods, turning over in his mind what he should do. For those who think this is an impossible dream for life in the twenty-first century, Eugene Peterson gives us the image of the pastor rising to his feet from idleness and not toil. This image derives from Peterson's notion of the 'unbusy pastor', a term that, as Ian Stackhouse says, looks like 'an oxymoron in our context'[6].

But this is in fact entirely in line with how, in every generation, we are intended to understand the Sabbath principle. Resting does not mean resignation or idleness, but suggests that we work *from* a place of rest rather than *towards* a place of rest. Our ability to stop what we are doing and be still before God is in fact an accurate indicator as to which direction our life is moving in, and where the source of our strength really lies.

Watchman Nee, the inspirational Chinese Church leader and writer, points out that however we interpret the Genesis 1 Creation account, Adam was created on the sixth day, so his first day was a day of rest – he began with a day off!

> Whereas God worked six days and then enjoyed his Sabbath rest, Adam began his life with the Sabbath; for God works before He rests, while man must first enter into God's rest, and then alone can he work.[7]

Thus, the day of rest is given not to recover from the demands of life and ministry in an over-busy week, but as a disengagement that can prepare us for a healthier re-entry into our life and leadership responsibilities. A true understanding of Sabbath is therefore not simply about heeding the external call for a day of rest, but the internal response that acknowledges our creaturely dependence on the Creator. It is in fact an act of faith, which many leaders find difficult, having got into a pattern of thinking that we can act out of our own wisdom and strength to solve the problems and achieve the goals we have set ourselves.

> No teaching flowing out of the Sabbath principle is more important than the centrality of our resting in God. Instead of striving to make this or that happen, we learn to trust in a heavenly Father who loves to give. This does not mean inactivity, but it does promote dependent activity. No longer do we take things into our own hands. Rather, we place all things into divine hands and then act out of inner promptings. (Richard Foster)[8]

Going back to the 'unbusy pastor', Peterson seems to suggest that the primary preoccupation of the leader should not be about 'making our mark'. Rather, it should be about ensuring, as Jesus did, that we are spending time with the Father. Through such commitment, given that the task of ministry has been helpfully described as 'the art of seeing well', we are then more likely to be able to discern what the Father is saying and doing (John 5:19).

Even when we recognise the importance of this kind of sight, many things can darken and cloud our eyes. It might be our own unmet needs or woundedness; it could be our self-interest, as opposed to the interests and needs of others; it may be a deep-down sense of disappointment or just sheer tiredness. The best way of addressing such feelings and emotions, however difficult this might be, is to make a commitment to building pools of stillness into our lives in order to allow the mud to settle and the waters to clear. The wise leader is the one who is courageous enough to stop, to wait, to listen; who thinks and feels and looks. As this happens, things begin to become a little clearer.

Speaking of his own practice in an interview with Nicky Gumbel, Vicar of Holy Trinity Brompton, Richard Chartres, Bishop of London had this to say:

> I don't honestly think there's any substitute for early hours. I don't think there's any substitute for chewing on Holy Scripture – and chewing, not in a tyrannical way that you're having all kinds of brilliant 'apercus and conceptions'. But chewing in the silence and the stillness. Regularity is so important. A time of silence and stillness; a time when one can be in God's presence. Orientated to God. Hearing the word in Holy Scripture and giving oneself sufficient relaxation to allow it to speak to us.[9]

In a similar vein, a lay person who has been a churchwarden in a number of different parishes, and has been sustained in their own discipleship through the disciplines of being a Benedictine Oblate, makes these observations:

> A fixed discipline of even 15 (better 30) minutes of personal prayer early in the day provides a launch-pad for the demanding routine of the parish cleric (or anyone else). It might seem a great deal to add on top of an already exhausting timetable. But in practice, such a commitment is a bedrock on which the rest of the day can be built, and from which the day will be easier.[10]

Especially when faced with significant demand and challenges, we must learn to recognise that leadership isn't just about the responsibilities we hold, having to make lots of decisions, or getting a great deal done:

> Leadership is about getting the right things done. As leaders, the crucial quality we need is the courage to stop. The courage to wait and be still. While everyone around

us is clamouring for a decision, the leader waits until she is confident and clear.[11]

Ken Blanchard is the author of *The One-Minute Manager* and a leading management consultant. In an article entitled 'Don't work harder – work smarter', he highlights one of the important lessons of leadership:

> Most people mentally have a sign over their desk that reads: Don't just sit there, do something! The best advice I ever received was to redo the sign to read: Don't just do something, sit there.[12]

Once more, the well-known words of Psalm 46 reveal God speaking at a time like our own, when society is in turmoil, even the most familiar landmarks are moving, and nothing seems certain anymore: 'Be still and know that I am God' (Ps. 46:10).

It seems there are some things that can only be learned in the secret and quiet place. Many things can be learned through activity and engagement with people, but a more intimate knowledge of God that will especially sustain us when the going is tough comes from an intentional commitment to stillness and silence. This shouldn't take us by surprise, because since God 'dwells in silence'[13], it follows that our deepest relationship with him will be in and through silence. We come to discover that often the most profound revelations come not through conscious thought, but simply by being in God's presence. Joyce Huggett describes contemplation and delight as the goal of silence:

> Contemplation goes further and deeper than meditation. While the person meditating mutters and muses on God's world, the contemplative pays silent attention to Jesus, the living Word – the one who is central to their prayer.[14]

In this sense, being still and listening, recognising that silence is part of the way and contemplation is both gift and goal, can be liberating. It helps us realise again that it is not so much a matter of us finding God in the busyness of our lives, as our being found by him. To embrace this can be a key step in the leader's own journey into healing and wholeness.

John Pritchard similarly puts his finger on the nub of the issue when he writes: 'Activism is a snare and delusion. We need time to think, reflect and pray.'[15]

The leader will have to be intentional about such a commitment to attentiveness – it won't happen by accident. It may mean a radical shift in mindset, seeing silence and reflection not as escapism from 'real ministry' nor the possession of a particular mood or emotion, but rather as an essential part of the resources for the real and often messy context that is human life.

Listening is valuable and restorative in itself, and is also the best way of discovering what our priorities should be, and of 'what the Spirit is saying to the church'.

Bishop Stephen Cottrell illustrates this with a medical analogy:

As any doctor will tell you, without a diagnosis there can never be a cure. Hence when you visit the doctor, you are the person to speak first. You describe your symptoms and your doctor listens carefully, probing you with questions, seeking to discover the precise nature of the problem. Only after that does your doctor offer a possible cure and even then a process of dialogue usually continues.[16]

THE LISTENING OF JESUS

It is clear from all the Gospel accounts, but especially that of Mark, that in Jesus' ministry there was a healthy pattern of engagement and reflection. In the opening six chapters of

Mark, we see an intense and demanding involvement with people – a ministry of healing, deliverance, preaching, training and equipping the twelve, as well as having to cope with misunderstanding, criticism and outright opposition. But this is balanced by a commitment to strategic withdrawal, marked by intentional reflection, prayer, fasting and solitude.

> In the morning, while it was still very dark, he got up and went out to a deserted place, and there he prayed. (Mark 1:35)

Despite the fact that people were continually looking for him, Jesus disciplined himself to be alone with his Father on a regular basis. Luke also describes the way in which he built this in to his life in these words:

> Yet the news about him spread all the more, so that crowds of people came to hear him and be healed of their sicknesses. But Jesus *often* withdrew to lonely places and prayed. (Luke 5:15–16)

When it came to the key decision-making process of choosing the twelve who would become apostles, he went up the mountain to pray:

> and called to him those whom he wanted and they came to him. And he appointed twelve whom he also named apostles, to *be with him* , and to be sent out to proclaim the message, and to have authority to cast out demons. (Mark 3:13–15)

He sent out the twelve on their first mission enterprise, and when they returned, he invited feedback from them: 'The apostles gathered around Jesus and told him all they had done and taught' (Mark 6:30).

No doubt there must have been plenty to talk about, because earlier in the chapter we read that as a result of their going and first attempts at proclamation, many people were healed and liberated. It would have been so tempting for Jesus at this point to send them on their way to continue what had clearly been fruitful and effective. But instead he said to them:

'Come away to a deserted place all by yourselves and rest a while'. For many were coming and going, and they had no leisure even to eat. And they went away in a boat to a deserted place by themselves. (Mark 6:31–32)

It is significant that the Greek word used here – *anapauo* – can mean rest in three ways: resting the body, soothing the soul and refreshing the spirit. What Jesus is instructing – not suggesting! – the disciples need at this point is renewal in every part of their being.

Echoing the wisdom of Jesus, it was St John Chrysostom who said: 'The bow that is never unstrung will quickly break.'

The next verses tell us that this stepping aside did not last for long, but I believe Jesus was seeking to model some principles for his disciples, that we neglect at our peril. At their heart is a commitment to stillness and listening. This was in part pragmatic, because like us, in his humanity, he got weary and stressed by the demands people put on him, and the expectations they had of him. Being alone was a way of recharging himself, of nourishing himself so he could give out to others. But this call to step aside was not simply for meeting the human need for rest, refreshment and relaxation; he wanted to keep intimate company with his Father, which would be his chief resource in the mission entrusted to him.

At the end of the prologue to John's Gospel, the author has this to say of the one who is the Word made flesh:

No one has ever seen God. It is God the only Son, *who is close to the Father's heart* who had made him known. (John 1:18)

Writing of the way in which Jesus guarded enough of his time so that he could maintain that intimacy, David Runcorn observes:

> His disciples discovered that this regular withdrawal from people and activity was the one predictable thing about Jesus. He made silence and solitude his special companions. Whatever the demands upon him, he always found a time and space to hide away and be alone.[17]

His mission was to do the Father's will, and it was in the secret, quiet place that he could hear the Father speak to him. Here, he knew himself to be accepted – reaffirming the public confirmation of his sonship, heard at his baptism and transfiguration, 'You are my Son whom I love' – and here that relationship would be sustained. Through that, in turn, his vision would be renewed, perspective restored and priorities realigned. Unlike many of us who are leaders today, Jesus would not allow any amount of busyness to rob him of the priority of sustaining oneness with the Father, even if the demands were insistent and seemed to be legitimate. He refused to settle for what one Christian leader described as 'a satisfactory working relationship with God'; he refused to sacrifice the vital for the pressing, the urgent for the important. Rather:

> In those lonely places the deep springs of the Spirit's life renewed him, the Father's will strengthened him and the Father's love inspired him ... Punctuation is a helpful way of thinking about Jesus' relationship with silence and solitude ... His times alone were the commas, pauses and full stops in the story of life. They gave the rest of life its structure, direction and balance. His words and works were born out of those silent hours of waiting upon God.[18]

WHY THEN DO WE AVOID SILENCE?

If withdrawal, and a commitment to periodic solitude that enabled silence and listening, were so important for Jesus, and so much in Christian tradition underlines the benefits for his disciples in their own journeys of faith and leadership responsibilities, why do we fail to commit to such times? Why this ambivalence of longing and yet at the same time avoidance?

For some, again particularly those of a more activist or extrovert disposition, silence, however much it may be longed for, can be far from easy. Our lives and ministries as leaders are filled with people, places and projects, and silence spells loneliness, which we dread. We identify with Martha when Jesus visited her and Mary in their home, 'distracted by all the preparations that have to be made … worried and upset about many things' (Luke 10:40–41). As a result, the body and mind finds it hard to slow down; there are all kinds of demands, real and imagined; voices whispering or even shouting 'this is a waste of time, you should be …'. We are thus left apprehensive rather than excited by the prospect of time alone – even with God.

Henri Nouwen recognised this ambivalence when he wrote: 'Solitude is both the place of great struggle and great encounter.'[19]

In the same book, he describes a time of withdrawal for Jesus where he certainly experienced this sense of struggle. During the forty days spent in the desert prior to the beginning of his public ministry, he faced three particular encounters with the devil understood by Nouwen as: temptations to be relevant, spectacular and powerful. Yet out of the desert struggle (which he would also experience at other times and places in his ministry, especially in the Garden of Gethsemane) comes great strength and insight, giving him the capacity to resist temptation and to know and do the Father's will.

To continue the 'desert metaphor', one reason we might find ourselves trying to avoid silence is because the desert, as Jesus found, is a place where we are confronted with our humanity in all its rawness, where we are simplified and stripped of all the non-essentials of life; it is a place of testing, refining and struggle, all of which might manifest themselves in different ways. Few would choose to be exposed in these areas. To put it another way, when the activity and noise cease, and we are alone before God, it is possible to feel very vulnerable, as we realise a sense of inner loneliness. Yet if we can stay with it, silence can come to be seen as a gift, part of a process by which we develop a greater dependence on and attachment to God, and less on ourselves and to other people. As one prayer helpfully puts it:

> Show me how to approach my sense of being alone and cut off so that it may not be any longer a condition to be dreaded, but rather seen as a means to closer dependence upon you. Let my soul learn in solitude the lesson of your presence.[20]

The Quaker tradition speaks of this kind of refining in the phrase 'the sifting silence'. This is again something we might not choose, but which in our better moments we know we need. Henri Nouwen describes this process, painful as it might feel, as one of the most positive outcomes of silence. For him it is the place where God can take away the false scaffolding of our lives:

> Silence is ... the place of conversion, the place where the old self dies and the new self is born, the place where the emergence of the new man and new woman occurs.[21]

Another reason we avoid silence is because it has within it the strong likelihood of waiting, and in twenty-first century culture we have little positive use for waiting. Much technology and expense today goes into reducing if not attempting to completely remove the waiting in our lives. It is a frustration, an annoyance, an intrusion, whether it is the failure of someone to reply immediately to an e-mail, or the wait in the doctor's surgery, at the bus stop or train station. Waiting interrupts our timetables, and delays our lives. I have no doubt that it has never been easy to 'wait for the Lord', a phrase found particularly in the Psalms, but expectations of instant response in the twenty-first century makes this doubly hard.

The image we have of God, and the basis on which we relate to him, may be a further reason for our ambivalence. No doubt the leader knows the 'theory' of God's nature and being, that 'we have received the spirit of adoption by which we cry "Abba, Father"'; we also know that he is 'for us and not against us' (Rom. 8:31). Nonetheless, if I am honest I can see in myself sometimes, as well as observing in others, a tendency to see God as an ever-demanding employer, who expects long hours. Or a God who is never satisfied even with our best efforts. Yes, even so-called mature Christian leaders can live with distorted images of God, and therefore be reluctant to spend time with him, in case even more will be expected. We may preach a Gospel of grace, but somehow can lose the reality of its truth in our own experience.

It is therefore vital for leaders to 'know themselves'. It may be true that some people have a natural preference for, and are renewed by, being alone and are drained by too much people contact. Others derive stimulation and energy from doing things and being with people. But all leaders, whatever their temperament and personality, need to find ways and means of replenishing their inner resources, for their own sakes and for the sake of those for whom they have responsibility.

Mother Teresa, as we know from more recent writings, herself struggled with the disciplines of prayer. Yet her words continue to speak into this call and challenge: 'The more we receive in silent prayer, the more we can give in our active life.'[22]

If we do find it hard to embrace stillness and silence, even to see its value, it is important that we recognise and acknowledge this. Rather than feeling guilty, or wishing we were 'wired up' in some different kind of way, we can instead find ways and means by which we can come to stillness. For some it may be listening to quiet, reflective, ambient music which brings us to that place; for others it may be walking, perhaps experimenting with what is sometimes described as a 'slow awareness walk', that helps to 'slow down the revs'. For others again, it may be keeping a spiritual journal. In my experience, this is one of the most helpful ways for any leader to learn to reflect, through tracing the activity of God in the day to day circumstances of our lives.

Practising this discipline over recent years has helped me greatly in this journey of self-understanding, as well as enabling me to better recognise the hand and 'voice' of God in my life and ministry.

Socrates is credited as saying that the unreflected life is not worth living, and Christian leaders down the centuries have clearly benefitted from the discipline of journaling. Some of these writings, like those of John Wesley or Soren Kierkegaard, have become spiritual classics. But we don't have to be in that league to discover the benefits of keeping a journal. Indeed, the last thing many of us would wish is to see our writings in print! Rather:

> Journalling helps us pay attention to God. It is a way of hearing and responding to God … For those who seek to follow Jesus, journals are an ideal way to track their journey and to interact with Jesus along the way. Journals help them to know themselves and God, and to see God at work in the intricacies of their lives.[23]

It is my conviction that understanding our different temperaments, rather than fighting the 'oughts' that bedevil many a leader's feelings about their relationship with God, is key to unlocking our capacity to hear God speak. This leads us to be able to intentionally build in realistic and appropriate disciplines, that will hopefully set us free for fresh encounter with the One who longs for our company. There may well be a need for persistence on our part, recognising that it can take time to quieten our minds and bodies and for the competing claims of attention to lose their sense of urgency.

Before leaving this issue of ambivalence, I observe that another reason that leaders often find it hard to be still enough to hear God, once more has to do with the issue of control. When we are truly listening to another person, and not imposing our thoughts, ideas and agendas, we are not in control in the same way as when we are speaking. When it comes to listening to God, the same is true. In effect we are saying the same thing as Samuel, when he finally came to understand it was the voice of the Lord calling in the night: 'Speak Lord, for your servant is listening' (1 Sam. 3:9). Articulating such a response, we are making ourselves vulnerable.

All of us use mechanisms of control in life, and at times these are entirely appropriate, for example in exercising control over a child about to run onto a busy main road. Control in itself is therefore not bad, and in times of crisis may be necessary and good. But it can also mask other things.

Simon Walker writes of a leader of a large and successful church struggling in this area of control:

> Here are some of the things Paul – not his real name – would say about himself. He finds it hard to be on his own. He finds it a challenge to pray privately and silently. He finds it hard to be doing nothing. He is tempted to avoid looking at the difficult stuff in his life. Other people would say of Paul that he is a fantastically confident, secure leader, always open to new opportunities, always looking forward.

The reasons why many leaders fear losing control, both in relation to other people but also to God, are varied and complex. It may be to do with an internal pressure to achieve standards and goals; it may be that in being still, as we have noted earlier, we are aware that we will have to face up to some failures, contradictions and compromises in our lives. Control in all its forms is one of the least acknowledged defences of the leader, and can prevent a capacity for inner stillness and receptivity to hearing and responding to the 'still small voice'. If there can be an honest acknowledgement of this, and perhaps a seeking of appropriate counsel and support, it is possible for the leader to come to a new place in which they are set free from seeking to meet personal needs and aspirations in unhelpful ways, and thereby to discover the possibility of healthier balance of engagement and reflection in their life.

I have discovered, (as many other leaders have, the hard way), that taking time apart is essential for a fruitful ministry. It is in the place of silence and solitude that ministry and spirituality meet each other. As we make space for God to speak, allowing him to continue his work of renewal and transformation within us, fresh insights will come, and fresh compassion will be born in us. We are better able to enter into others' pain and vulnerability, because we have not run away from our own pain and vulnerability. We can understand others' brokenness because we have had to face our own. So it is that in coming apart, we are not moving away from or avoiding people; rather we will be better able to identify with, and potentially speak more helpfully to, their needs and aspirations.

For almost six years, I was Warden of the Lee Abbey community in North Devon, and we were fortunate to have another religious community on our doorstep – the Roman Catholic order of the Fransiscan Poor Clares. Theirs is essentially a call to the contemplative life, with few of the sisters having emerged into the 'outside world' for many years. Yet what I discovered through my contact with them was that, alongside a great sense of fun and a keen awareness of what is going on in the world, they were in tune with and have extraordinary insights into contemporary culture. Yes, they watched the news once a day, but theirs was an understanding fed by silence and contemplation; it was a listening to 'the signs of the times'. This kind of 'seeing' and listening under-pins all effective leadership, not simply because of what is 'seen', but the way it is seen.

> Action is the stream, and contemplation is the spring ... it is for us to take care that these living waters well up in our own hearts. God will make it his concern to guide our action if we live in him, and he will turn the stream to whatever channels he wills ... when action and contem-plation dwell together, filling our whole life because we are moved in all things by the Spirit of God, then we are spiritually mature. (Thomas Merton)[25]

THE SILENCE OF GOD

Matters of temperament, fear of the 'desert place', the chal-lenge of waiting, distorted images of God and the need to control are all reasons why we may avoid stillness. This chapter would be incomplete, however, if alongside those, we did not also acknowledge that at times, however much we put ourselves in a place of listening, God seems to choose silence. 'What is the point of being still, when silence feels like absence and emptiness?' is a question that may at some point be as much part of the journey of faith for a Christian leader as for anyone else. Theologians have a phrase to describe this: '*Deus absconditus*' – the God who is hidden.

Many would identify with C. S. Lewis when he wrote, following the death of his beloved wife, Joy:

> Meanwhile, where is God? This is one of the most disquieting symptoms. When you are happy, so happy

you have no sense of needing him, if you turn to him with praise, you will be welcomed with open arms. But go to him when your need is desperate, when all other help is vain and what do you find? A door slammed in your face and a sound of bolting and double bolting on the inside. After that *silence* (my italics). You may as well turn away.[26]

Lewis' experience is mirrored by that of Job in the Old Testament. Through his suffering and loss, Job asks whether a person who suffers undeservedly can continue to believe that a silent God is a just God. From this position, Job indicts God, wants his questions answered and demands that God justifies his actions. But all he hears are 'the sounds of silence'. It seems a tough lesson. God, it seems, is not obliged to explain his silence. Eventually, after thirty-seven chapters of silence, we hear, as it were, God's side of the story – he speaks out of the whirlwind:

'Who is this that darkens my counsel with words without knowledge? Brace yourself like a man; I will question you, and you shall answer me.' (Job 38:2–3)

Hardly the answer Job would have wanted or expected, as God doesn't actually answer his questions. In fact he has a list of questions for Job! At first sight, this response seems both insensitive and irrelevant. It can read as though God acts like a judge who has dozed off in the middle of a trial, and thereby has missed the main argument! Finally, having listened to what God has to say, Job gets the opportunity to reply:

'I know you can do all things; no plan of yours can be thwarted. You asked "Who is this that obscures my counsel without knowledge?" Surely I spoke of things I did not understand, things too wonderful for me to know … My ears had heard of you but now my eyes have seen you.' (Job 42:2–4)

In other words, Job may not have understood the reasons why he and his family had to endure so much, or why God seemed silent for such a long time, but in the revelation that eventually came, he was content to live with the fact that God's purposes are sometimes hidden. It was Blaise Pascal who said: 'A religion that does not affirm God is sometimes hidden is not true.'

As well as desperately painful times, when the hidden-ness of God truly does feel more like absence, there are times in ministry which feel plain humdrum and ordinary; when we are working away and there appear to be no visible results. There are no major crises for us or for others, but God's voice seems to be so quiet as to be inaudible. What might be termed the 'usual' ways of listening and encounter do not seem to be effective.

David Runcorn (again in his *Space for God*) has some helpful insights for times like this. He suggests we may have to be prepared to 'let go of God', by which he means recognising that we don't own him; that we have no rights over him. Sometimes, as I have already suggested, it can be a false, inadequate or even distorted picture of God which is blocking our hearing. If we are prepared to do any necessary 'letting go', this can create space to allow a fuller and truer vision of God to come. It may not happen immediately; there may well be a difficult period when there is no apparent sense of God at all. What the leader will need to do then, in part alone – but some of the journey can be shared with others he or she can confide in – is to hang on, drawing on the reservoir of what has been known of God in the past, until, hopefully in a deeper and more profound way, there is a conscious sense of encounter once more.

It is possible to come to understand silence and the apparent absence of God as friend not foe; not as a blockage but as a potential means of leading to a deeper sense of trust, and thereby a better discernment of God's will and priorities.

Oswald Chambers puts it this way:

> Has God trusted you with his silence – a silence that has great meaning? God's silences are actually his answers. Just think of those days of absolute silence in the home at Bethany! (John 11.6) ... Are you mourning before God because you have not had an audible response? When you cannot hear God, you will find that he has trusted you in the most intimate way possible – with absolute silence, not a silence of despair, but one of pleasure, because he saw you could withstand an even bigger revelation.[27]

Teresa of Avila described one silent stage in the mystic journey as 'the Prayer of Quiet'. In it, the inner senses fade into silent dark communion with God, and we do not feel the need for inner sights and sounds, as all becomes absolute stillness. We know God is there, not because of anything our senses tell us, but through sheer, raw faith. Our spirits are joined with God's Spirit, bearing witness that we are children of God (Rom. 8:16). Here is part of Teresa's description of a silence of God that is actually a rich, authentic state of prayer:

> This is a supernatural state, and however hard we try, we cannot reach it for ourselves; for it is a state in which the soul enters into peace, or rather in which the Lord gives it peace through his presence, as he did to that just man Simeon (Luke 2:25–35). In this state, all the faculties are stilled. The soul, in a way which has nothing to do with the outward senses, realises that it is now very close to its God and that, if it were but a little closer, it would become one with him through union. This is not because it sees him either with its bodily or with its spiritual eyes ... It is, as it were, a swoon, both inwardly and

outwardly, so that the outward man (let me call it the 'body', and then you will understand me better) does not wish to move, but rests, like one who has almost reached the end of his journey, so that it may the better start again upon its way, with redoubled strength for the task.[28]

St John of the Cross (1542–1591), looks beyond the Prayer of Quiet into more of the sense of struggle with which I began this section – a deeper and apparently darker silence that he called 'the Dark Night of the Soul'. He speaks of the Dark Night of the Soul as that stage on the mystical path when:

spiritual persons suffer great trials, by reason not so much of the aridities (dryness) which they can suffer, as of the fear which they have of being lost on the road, thinking that all spiritual blessing is over for them and that God has abandoned them since they find no help or pleasure in good things.[29]

Through this process, hard and unwelcome as it may seem, faith is refined (1 Pet. 1:7): 'to come to a pleasure you know not, you must go by a way you enjoy not'. According to John, this makes possible a work of radical transformation deep within one's spirit. The true 'dark night' of which he speaks is not to be confused with depression, or apathy. No amount of medication, counselling or spiritual direction will break this silence.

As leaders, if we risk disclosing to others, however appropriately, that this is a season we are currently experiencing, we may run the risk of some questioning both our spirituality and our fitness for leadership. However, if this is a time through which we are travelling, it is important we find those we can trust with whom to share the reality of what is going on for us. Furthermore, experience seems to suggest that sometimes all we can do is submit to it, and wait for God to complete his work, rather as a chrysalis has to wait for the inner metamorphosis that results in a butterfly. We can't force the pace, but the end result of what can feel like a silent affliction rather than a gift, is a process of purification that can bring that inner freedom to which I referred earlier, that desire for oneness with God, which in the mystical tradition is sometimes referred to as 'Love Union'.

This is where we come to understand that God's apparent silence and purposes are not to wound or hurt, but part of the journey to wholeness, and 'closeness to the Father's heart'. Along with those who may perceive the leaders experiencing this season as something negative, there will equally be those for whom it is a relief to know that their leader is human too, and who recognise the fruit that emerges 'in due season'.

Chapter four

Learning to listen to those from whom we differ

Obedience demands of you
That you listen to the other person;
Not only to what he is saying
But to what he is.
Then you will begin to live in such a way
That you neither crush nor dominate
Nor entangle your brother
But help him to be himself,
And lead him to freedom. ('Rule For a New Brother')[1]

Listening to others is perhaps the hardest work in which we will ever engage, but it results in our discovery of their loveableness, hidden though it may sometimes be under successive layers of repellent distortion. (Harry Williams)[2]

These two quotations from very different sources powerfully illustrate both the importance and challenge of listening to others. They suggest the consequent freedom and new insights that can emerge, when we are not afraid to acknowledge difference, coming to see it more as a stepping stone than a stumbling block.

This aspect of the listening process begins with the *verbal* – listening to what is actually said, not least to emphases, inconsistencies, evasions, likes and dislikes, fears, joys and sorrows.

It notices and takes into account the *non-verbal* – body language; what lies behind what is said; being aware of facial expressions, ways of sitting, eyes, hands and tone of voice.

This kind of listening also involves *our own reactions* – listening to ourselves; keeping a watch on how we feel about what we are hearing. It is aware of whether our own experience is cutting in unhelpfully. We reduce the quality of our listening when we start to make comparisons (spoken or unspoken) with a similar situation – our own or someone else's.

High quality listening is, I would suggest, in short supply, both in the world in general, and also in the Church, including among its leaders. That is especially so in the context of dealing with difference. As we have seen in other chapters, in one way there is nothing new about this. It seems to me that the tendency for difference to lead to division has its roots in what we see described in the narrative of the third chapter of Genesis. As we continue to read through the pages of Scripture, there is example after example of this happening between individuals, and within the life of the people of God. But in every generation, there are also factors, particularly in wider society, that affect how the Church, and its leaders, engage with difference.

COMPETITION VERSUS CO-OPERATION

In these first years of the twenty-first century, two apparently contradictory things seem to be happening at the same time. On one hand, the world appears to be fragmenting into smaller pieces, leading to the emergence of self-interested groupings, large and small, of the like-minded – whether that manifests itself in political, economic or religious alliances. On the other, we are being thrust closer together, not only as a result of instant communication, possible now in ways unimagined even a few decades ago, but also because of some of the common problems that confront us day by day. A major illustration of this would be in the environmental challenges we face. In particular climate change, with the consequent threats posed by melting ice-caps, changing weather systems and warming oceans. Dave Bookless, the UK Director of A Rocha, in his book *Planetwise*, speaks of 'the terrible effects these will have indeed are already having, on wildlife, the poor and ultimately, all of us.'[3]

He goes on in the same chapter to speak of how we are all affected by the destruction of forests, the over-fishing of oceans and dangerous pesticides and chemicals causing huge problems to eco systems and human health.

From this, and many other examples that could be given, we recognise that how we live and act in one place has consequences for others – it affects the whole. As we have experienced from the autumn of 2008 onwards, the actions and policies (or, some would say, the lack of action and appropriate policies), of a relatively small group of people charged with financial responsibilities led to global recession, with consequences for everyone, especially the poorest and most marginalised.

The words of the seventeenth century metaphysical poet John Donne, later to become Dean of St Paul's Cathedral, contain a timeless truth in this connection: 'Every man's death diminishes me, for I am a human being.'

Difference, then, it seems, can lead us in one of two directions – towards an increased competitiveness that can lead to mistrust and division, or to the open recognition of difference, and the possibility of understanding and even co-operation. True co-operation, however, requires a commitment to listening: a quality of listening that can turn strangers into friends. This is a listening that recognises and celebrates difference, whilst being concerned to maintain the integrity of 'the other'; which recognises that if we were totally the same, we would have nothing to say to each other!

SOME KEY AREAS OF DIFFERENCE FOR THE TWENTY-FIRST CENTURY CHURCH

It seems to me that the two apparent contradictions outlined above are also being played out in the life of the Church, which makes the task of leadership, at whatever level, especially challenging. As we wrestle with theological, ecclesiological and ethical issues, we see all around us evidence of fragmentation, and the consequent formation of various alliances. (I will illustrate here mainly from the Anglican context because this is where I have been called into leadership and thereby know it best. However, there are equivalent tensions and areas of disagreement in other traditions and denominations. One example would be when the Roman Catholic Church found itself in a state of disarray after 'Humanae Vitae', though it could be argued that they had better ecclesiological tools to deal with the disagreement.)

To take the matter of the ordination of women to the priesthood (and already in some parts of the Anglican Communion, and potentially in others, to the Episcopate), there are those that hold a strongly sacramental view of priesthood who do not believe Christ can be represented by a woman at the altar. Furthermore, they believe that decisions in recent years to ordain women have broken with centuries of church tradition and further impaired, if not broken, relationships, especially with the Roman Catholic and Orthodox communions.

There are others whose reading of the Scriptures and interpretation of some passages in the Pauline epistles leads them to the conviction that, on the grounds of headship, it is inappropriate for a woman to inhabit the office of priest or bishop.

Talking to friends and colleagues who hold leadership responsibilities in the church and who hold these views on women in such leadership roles – views which I respect and take seriously, even though I may not agree with them – I find that though they occupy some common ground on the matter of women in leadership, they do so on little else in terms of theology or church order. All too often – though happily there are exceptions, such as in the Diocese of Manchester where there have been regular meetings and opportunities for prayer and ongoing conversation together between, among others, the Women's Chapter, and members of Forward in Faith – what I notice is that, rather than an ongoing commitment to true listening to others with differing viewpoints, people simply defend their own position in a way that can only lead to further fragmentation and division.

Martyn Percy, writing on the subject of gender and change, makes this comment:

> The debate about women bishops highlights the strengths and weaknesses of the Anglican Church and its attempt to reach consensus on almost any matter. In a church where compromise has often had to form the basis for communion, and where competing convictions have sometimes threatened to tear the church apart, the debate offers a genuine opportunity to recover the charity that Anglicans need to live together as faith disciples, yet also as those who do not agree on certain matters of faith and order.[4]

Earlier in the same book he observes that:

> Only when the intense heat of the arguments that bedevil it begin to cool, can Anglicanism recover its poise, and its members start talking and listening to one another rather than shouting.[5]

A lack of commitment to genuine listening in any area of life can blind us to the full consequences of our actions. At the 2008 Lambeth Conference of Bishops, a number of bishops from the Episcopal Church of the USA commented at the time that, had they realised the effect and impact on the world-wide Communion of ordaining someone a bishop whose sexual orientation and practice was homosexual, 'we might have voted differently at the election'. This wasn't necessarily that their convictions would have changed; as they see it, and subsequent decisions in the Episcopal Church have confirmed this, for many in that church it is a matter of justice to offer gay and lesbian people who are in partnerships a full inclusion in the church's life and leadership which they believe has been hitherto denied to them. Nonetheless, in conversations among a significant number of bishops at the conference, there was a recognition that the theological, ecclesiological and ethical implications of such a decision may not have been sufficiently thought through as far as the world-wide Anglican Communion is concerned.

Commenting on further developments, including the over-turning of the agreed moratoria on the part of the Episcopal Church in subsequently electing bishops in same sex partner-ships, the Bishop of London, the Rt Revd Richard Chartres, wrote in the summer of 2009:

> Now what has happened in the United States is that there has been a tendency to move ahead with a very provincial understanding of Christian truth – without *listening deeply* (italics mine), without consulting others – in something which concerns the whole Church.[6]

Whatever one's viewpoint on the issue itself, the point here is that these steps have further exacerbated tensions with others within the Episcopal Church who would describe themselves as conservative or orthodox, causing some of them to see no alternative but to leave and set up alternative provision, as well as the effects felt within the wider Anglican Commun-ion. In this context, for some, it may be that the Pope's 'generous offer' in the late autumn of 2009 to the 'Traditional Anglican Communion', and others who in various ways would call themselves traditionalists (the Apostolic Constitu-tion, 'Anglicanorum Coetibus'), might offer a way out of their dilemma. This came as a result of requests to the Pope from some Bishop and others in this constituency for full Communion with Rome, without preconditions or demands, while expressing the hope that it might be possible to retain Anglican orders, liturgy and hymnody. As I write, it is unclear how many in the Anglican Communion will take this route. While it may meet the needs of some, there are many who hope that there may continue to be a place in the Anglican Church and Communion which they can occupy with integrity. The danger is that patience on all sides seems to be running, or, as some would say, has run, out, which is why the Archbishop of Canterbury's speech to the General Synod of February 2010 on the 'patient quest for living together in mutual charity, even while we disagree' was so important. Commenting on this, George Guiver, Superior of the Community of the Resurrection at Mirfield, wrote:

> In the present very polarised situation in the church, it is not possible to try and sit on the fence –there is no middle ground. What is possible is a respect for each other of the kind Rowan described in his speech. The Gospel is not about winning battles over brothers and sisters, but the hard struggle to hold everyone together in love. We and other religious communities firmly believe this is possible; and the way to it is not by smudging or avoiding matters of difference, but by being open with each other while, in St Benedict's words, 'honouring one another'.[7]

The question that we have to wrestle with is well-expressed by Oliver O'Donovan, albeit referring mainly to the area of sexuality, but I believe applicable more widely in areas of significant difference of conviction:

> What room is there for a 'pluralism' in the church's moral beliefs and practice, i.e., the acceptance of tolerable but ethically significant difference? Such an acceptance will not be possible, we must assume, when moral

difference reflects significant doctrinal disagreement, bringing the common Christian faith into question.[8]

THE CHURCH AND OTHER FAITH COMMUNITIES

As I briefly noted at the end of Chapter One, there are similarly potentially choppy waters being navigated when it comes to relationships between Christianity and other faiths. In twenty-first century life in the UK, increasing numbers of Christians encounter people from other faith communities on a daily basis. This may be as their neighbours, work colleagues, people who serve them in local shops or through their children where schools have a significant mixture of people from other faith backgrounds.

Although I referred to four possible approaches to relationships between Christians and those of other faiths, another way of looking at it is in terms of two basic schools of thought when it comes to inter-religious dialogue. One approach is dedicated (more or less subtly!), to the conversion of people to Christ, the unique revelation of God, from whatever their original religious tradition and background. The second sees Christians as witnesses to the revelation of God in Christ, but approaches other faith traditions as valid manifestations of the divine. In more recent years there are many who would challenge this 'either/or' approach, that reduces relationships to *either* direct evangelism *or* inter-faith dialogue.

In 2005, the Mission and Public Affairs Council of the Church of England published its report 'Presence and Engagement: the churches task in a multi Faith society'[9]. This report sought to take into account the changes affecting the interfaith scene in the light of 9–11, and the key role many parish clergy played along with faith leaders generally in keeping their communities together. But it also highlighted the demographic changes that were affecting the ministry and mission of parishes in the inner areas of our major towns and cities. Important questions were asked, and in-depth research carried out on what it means for an Anglican parish church to be 'there' for all people (presence), when in some parishes anywhere between 50 and 90+ per cent of the people belonged to communities of faith other than Christian. The title of the report is a positive and succinct way of both expressing a dilemma and a commitment. As the late Bishop John Austin, then Chair of the Inter-Faith Consultative Group, put it: 'Within the providence of God there is nothing to fear in this process. There is only enrichment as the responses to our questionnaires reveal.'

Despite this work, and the more recently published and well-received document 'Generous Love: the truth of the Gospel and the call to dialogue', both at local and national levels difference of attitude and practice can still lead Christians to take up very different positions, sadly sometimes fuelled by ignorance, prejudice or rumour. As a result, it is hard for those in leadership roles to help people 'celebrate difference and stay faithful' with integrity.

THE IMPORTANCE OF DIALOGUE

It may be that these problems are in part a result of an inadequate understanding of the word 'dialogue'. Martin Goldsmith, recognising that Christians can sometimes be fearful or reluctant to learn from those of other faiths, has this to say:

> Dialogue may be defined as a form of communication which does not only indulge in a monologue declaration of the Gospel. Dialogue must include the opportunity for all involved to share their beliefs and feelings. This means that dialogue always takes the form of a discussion or debate rather than a one-sided proclamation which allows no sharing, questioning or disagreement from the listener.[10]

In the Keele Evangelical Congress of 1967, dialogue was defined as a situation where 'each party ... desires to listen and learn as well as to speak and instruct.' Listening and learning thus constitute a vital part of dialogue.

But as we see from the different ways in which the word dialogue is used in the New Testament, it is clear that such listening and learning should not preclude speaking or proclamation. There are actually three Greek variants of the Greek word for dialogue: *dialogizomai*, and the related *dialogismos*, seem to have the sense of questioning and uncertain thinking, while *dialogomai* seems to contain the more definite idea of arguing, reasoning and contending. In the Acts of the Apostles, Luke only uses one of these words – *dialogomai* – and in Acts 17:2 and 17:17, the RSV translates this as 'argued'. However, within the passage as a whole, the impression given is that Paul in a masterly way combines a listening to the context of Athens and its people and an appropriate proclamation of the good news of Jesus Christ, culminating in the message of resurrection (*anastasia* in the original Greek). In the light of this, it seems that true dialogue can and should involve a mixture of listening, debating and proclamation. But, as Kenneth Cragg expressed it in his book, *Sandals at the Mosque*:

> Dialogue in the sense of a reverent, tactical, tender and sensitive approach is not merely to be argued for on a 'tactical score', but also because it reflects a genuine and humble concern for the other person. If our manner of preaching does not convey a Christ-like love and humility, then our lives actually preach a false gospel even if our words remain utterly Biblical.[11]

THE ISSUE OF AUTHORITY

We have to recognise that underlying the areas touched on so far, as well as others where difference can potentially lead to division, is the issue of authority, and in particular the authority, place and interpretation of Scripture.

Again to quote O'Donovan:

> Authority is what evokes belief and obedience, and questions of belief and obedience are all, at root, moral questions – not in the superficial sense of being related to the details of our behaviour, but as concerned with the ways we dispose of ourselves in our living ... obedience is a duty that needs the discipline of hermeneutic reflection if it is to be carried through. We cannot 'obey' in a vacuum of understanding.[12]

So for example, when it comes to same sex relationships, the 'traditional' approach would broadly be concerned to faithfully pass on to the next generation what has been passed on to us, in terms of Scripture and Tradition, as reflected, for example, in the wording of the Preface read by the bishop prior to Anglican clergy taking their Oaths and Declarations:

> The Church of England is part of the One, Holy, Catholic and Apostolic Church, worshipping the one true God, Father, Son and Holy Spirit. It professes the faith uniquely revealed in the Holy Scriptures and set forth in the catholic creeds, which faith the Church is called upon to proclaim afresh in each generation.

This wording involves an acknowledgement that the Gospel has to continually be freshly contextualised, but equally at the very least implies that Scripture and tradition hold 'givens' beyond which it is not appropriate to go, both in terms of belief and practice. Thus, the wording continues:

> Led by the Holy Spirit, it has borne witness to Christian truth in its historical formularies, the Thirty Nine Articles of Religion, the Book of Common Prayer and the Order-

ing of Bishops, Priests and Deacons. In the declaration you are about to make, will you affirm your loyalty to this inheritance of faith as your inspiration and guidance under God in bringing the grace and truth of Christ to this generation and making Him known to those in your care?

It seems to me that at the heart of the Gospel is a genuine welcome to all, 'come as you are', but, equally, a challenge to every individual to embrace change and transformation in conformity to God's will as revealed in the Scriptures, Creeds and Traditions of the Church. Such an understanding is illustrated by an example such as Jesus' words to the woman caught in the act of adultery, and consequently experiencing humiliation at the hands of some of the Scribes and Pharisees. Having taken time to reflect in response to their persistent attempts to trap him and destroy her, Jesus says: 'Let anyone among you who is without sin be the first to throw a stone at her.'

As they slope off, unable to rise to that challenge, after a further pause to reflect, Jesus speaks to the woman in these words:

'Woman, where are they? Has no one condemned you?' She said, 'No one sir'. And Jesus said, 'Neither do I condemn you. Go your way, and from now on do not sin again.' (John 8:10–11)

Similarly St Paul, having spent the first eleven chapters of the Letter to the Romans describing all that God has accomplished in Christ, in Chapter 12 moves to demonstrate how doctrine is to be translated into practice, and does so with these words:

Do not be conformed to this world (age), but be transformed by the renewing of your minds, so that you can discern what is the will of God – what is good and acceptable and perfect.' (Rom. 12:2)

The Greek verb for 'transformed' is *metamorphoo*, which is the same as the word translated 'transfigure' in the transfiguration narratives of Matthew 17 and Mark 9. The only other place it appears in the New Testament is 2 Corinthians 3:18, where it speaks of believers being 'changed' into the likeness of Christ 'from one degree of glory to another' through the work of the 'Lord who is the Spirit'.

Recognising the danger of caricature either way, what is often called a more 'liberal inclusive' approach to sexuality might be expressed in words like these, from one church leader with whom I was in conversation:

> Having experienced almost forty years of life, love, companionship and faithfulness in a Christian marriage, who am I to deny that to people who experience same sex attraction? For me this is not primarily a sexual issue, but a relational one. I am not wanting to encourage promiscuity, but to honour commitment.

Or from another conversation in which I was involved:

> It's my conviction that Jesus is alive in the hearts, minds and contexts of where people are now. People who are gay and lesbian are at risk in society, and the church should be the place above all where they are welcome and accepted as they are.

Putting the question in the area of same-sex relationships quite starkly, as far as issues of authority and tradition are concerned: is 'inclusion' and the acceptance of those relationships at the same level as the heterosexual, a development or a deviation?

Whether in the area of same-sex relationships or of inter-religious dialogue, or indeed any other where there is potential for serious difference of belief to lead to division, another question to be wrestled with is: is the Holy Spirit taking us into 'new truth' or calling us to fresh obedience to 'old truth'? Or again, to take the words of the Declaration and Oaths, how do we interpret the phrase 'proclaim afresh'? How are the grace and truth of Christ to be brought to this generation?

One of the realities for leaders seeking to handle these areas of difference is that, rightly and understandably, we have come to our own often strongly-held convictions. But we also need to recognise that along with those well thought-through and deeply held convictions may also be some prejudices fuelled by our own experience, temperament and personality. Given this, how do we handle ourselves, seeking to maintain our own integrity, as well as trying to equip other people to deal with difference constructively, because challenging issues of whatever kind are not going to go away.

GIVING WAY OR GIVING IN?

As I have reflected on this in my own ministry, and from observation of others, at a quite basic level, I believe we often confuse *acceptance* and *agreement*, or, to use a road sign analogy, *giving way* and *giving in*.

I am a parent of two – now grown-up – sons. I am deeply grateful for the warm, trusting and open relationship we enjoy, but I would be less than honest if I said that I had agreed with every decision they had taken, every item of clothing they had worn, every taste in music, every place they'd gone or every friend they had made in earlier years! But even if there wasn't agreement, I hope and believe it didn't make any difference to the acceptance and love I had for them. Acceptance and agreement are not the same.

Similarly, as someone with considerable experience of leadership in local church life, as well as now painting on a 'broader canvas', I have seen many instances in parochial church councils and other church meetings, where people were clearly afraid that to *give way* on a point would be like *giving in* – a sign of weakness and defeat. And yet, why do we have *give way* signs? Is it not in order to stop unnecessary accidents and crashes; to enable people to pause before moving on safely?

Along with these respective potential confusions, I believe that as leaders we need to be more ready to acknowledge our own fears, where they have come from, and what over the years has shaped our thinking – the good things – but also what has tainted or even polluted us. Real listening means that we encounter the person and not just the argument, but sadly, sometimes, because of what has coloured our own past we are capable of making a judgement from what is in reality a knee-jerk reaction or prejudice. Within all this too, we have to recognise our own cultural conditioning.

Another example from Jesus' ministry that illustrates this is in his encounter with the Syro-Phoenician woman, described in Mark 7:24–30. In his humanity, it could be argued that Jesus displayed a culturally-conditioned attitude – what might have been called the divinely ordained division between the people of Israel and the Gentiles – but through his compassionate listening, he turned a potential stumbling-block into a stepping stone.

PRINCIPLES AND A FRAMEWORK FOR LISTENING

I believe as leaders we need some principles and a framework that will enable us and those for whom we have responsibility to truly learn to listen to those from whom we differ. We need means by which stereotypical thinking is broken down, and whereby we are open to the possibility of changing some of our own thought forms and understandings, while at the same time maintaining our own integrity.

To return to the 2008 Lambeth Conference, for a considerable time before it began it was clear that here was great potential for matters of difference to lead to further fragmentation and division within the Anglican Communion. The presenting issue was in the area of human sexuality, and specifically that of the decision in 2003 of the Episcopal Church of the USA to ordain Gene Robinson, who was in a same-sex partnered relationship, as Bishop of New Hampshire.

In 2007, the then head of the Anglican Church in Nigeria, Archbishop Peter Akinola, indicated that he would boycott the Lambeth Conference unless the US Church halted what he called its 'liberal agenda', especially on the issue of homosexuality. A quote from an article in *The Times*, of 5 July 2007, put it like this:

> Dr Akinola has lost faith that the Episcopal Church of the United States, which precipitated a schism with the ordination of the gay Bishop, Gene Robinson in 2003, will ever *listen* to the conservative evangelical leaders of the Global South churches of Africa and Asia.

On the other hand, there was correspondence at the same time, from within the gay and lesbian communities in some countries in Africa and Asia, that the stance of Archbishop Akinola and others was putting their lives at risk.

When it came to the Lambeth Conference itself, because there was no change in the position of the Episcopal Church, Archbishop Akinola and a significant number of other primates and bishops chose not to come to Canterbury. (This despite the fact that Bishop Gene Robinson himself was not invited by the Archbishop of Canterbury.) Their non-attendance was something that saddened the Archbishop deeply, along with the majority of those who attended – myself included. However, the note sounded at the beginning of the conference was a positive one, as Archbishop Rowan spoke of his conviction of a future with hope for the Anglican Communion – a conviction he retains notwithstanding the ways in which events have moved on since – in these words from the opening presidential address: 'Whatever the popular perception, the options before us are not irreparable schism or forced assimilation.'

Despite that, the prospects were not good for the conference, and many inside and beyond the Church predicted that the whole experience would be at best a waste of time and money, and at worst the death knell of the Anglican Communion. One of the key reasons the conference proved to be neither – which is in no way to minimise the tensions that remain, and indeed have increased since, nor how deeply issues were and are felt – was because of the 'Indaba process' that would characterise the whole gathering. It would be inaccurate if I did not acknowledge that some participants felt that this approach 'fudged' some of the areas of difference and potential division. However, I believe there are some insights and principles from this process that infused the whole conference which are transferrable, and can help those who are leaders understand some principles in learning to listen to those from whom we differ. These are insights which seem to me not only to be applicable at every level of church life, but also in any areas of family, community or work life, wherever there is difference to be faced.

THE INDABA PROCESS – A FRAMEWORK FOR LISTENING

The concept of Indaba is based on an African ideal of purposeful discussion on the common concerns of shared life. It is a process and method of engagement, unrushed and participatory, that enables people with different perspectives to truly listen to 'the other'. An Indaba acknowledges first and foremost that there are issues that need to be addressed effectively to 'foster ongoing communal living'. I believe this is important. My experience of local church life suggests to me that sometimes the reason there is conflict, disharmony and division in the present is because difference was not faced and addressed constructively in the past. Either it was unresolved and hostilities remain, the same issues being played out with a different cast, or it was 'pushed under the carpet', so either way, a legacy of 'wounded history' is left.

The aim of an Indaba process is to enable every person to truly listen, as well as to bring their perspective and speak their mind. Those in leadership roles or who are more articulate or powerful in personality have no particular privilege. It is about a person-to-person encounter that can enable everyone to move forward with integrity.

As background to an effective 'Indaba approach', there needs to be the acknowledgement that effective listening emerges from the recognition that every human being is created in the image and likeness of God. Without that commitment to honour others' humanity, dialogue – the meaning of which we have already examined – is unlikely to get very far. Also to be borne in mind is that the purpose of listening is not to compromise, but to grow in trust and understanding of the 'other's' traditions and convictions. In this sense we are talking about listening as hospitality, as in the Benedictine tradition whereby hospitality is seen in part as making space in our hearts for 'the other'. As Henri Nouwen has expressed it:

> Hospitality is not to change people, but to offer them space where change can take place ... hospitality is not a subtle invitation to adopt the lifestyle of the host, but a chance for the guest to find his own.[13]

The aim of the planning group of the Lambeth Conference was that every aspect should be an expression of Indaba, whether in the worship, daily Bible studies, hearings or plenary sessions; indeed, even in conversations in meal queues and the bars! But much of the deeper dialogue took place in designated groups. I was part of an Indaba group helpfully facilitated as '*animateur*' by a bishop from South Africa. He had experience of, understood and valued the process 'from the inside'. (Depending on the context, where there are issues of significant difference, it can help to have someone who is a 'neutral outsider' facilitating dialogue and conversation.)

As I experienced the process, I found myself asking what difference such an approach might make to the way as a Church we deal with difference, not just at international or national level but in the diocesan or local context. Could it apply whether the potentially divisive issues are theological, ecclesiological, ethical or downright practical, such as new pastoral arrangements, church building re-ordering schemes, or styles and times of services in a local parish?

Let me outline some of the insights at the heart of the Indaba process. Five 'ground rules' were set out:

1. Listen sincerely, and speak with integrity.
2. It is acceptable to disagree, but this runs alongside a commitment to maintain relationship and respect of others' viewpoints.
3. It is important to speak in the first person.
4. This process is not about 'win/lose'.
5. We must each ask ourselves the question: 'What sacrifices am I prepared to make, and what generous initiatives might I take, in order to move things forward?'

Looking at these 'ground rules', I ask again what impact might it have on our dealing with difference, if there were a commitment to approaching issues in this way? It does require a willingness on the part of all concerned to make this 'work', but the initiative needs to start with those of us entrusted with leadership responsibilities.

LISTENING IN INTER-FAITH CONTEXTS

In order to see how this might work out in practice, let me return to one of the areas of 'difference' alluded to earlier, namely that of the relationship between Christianity and other faiths. As leaders, we have a responsibility to encourage initiative-taking in this area.

How effective listening happens will of course be affected by the context of the conversation, and those with whom we are in dialogue. For example, a conversation with people from the Jewish or Muslim communities where we hold a monotheistic faith in common will be different in its starting point from our listening with people from a Hindu or Sikh background. (An illustration of this is the Muslim document *Common Word*, in which 'Love of God and love for neighbour' are identified as the two common starting points for listening and working together.) I am aware of course that Christians in some situations are being faced with discrimination, hostility, or even persecution on the part of (albeit extreme) members of other faith groups. The reality is that for some, entering into the kind of listening process I am describing would be at best difficult, certainly dangerous and sometimes impossible.

That said, where there is the possibility of effective listening, in inter-faith contexts, the following might be practical ways for Christians of putting Indaba principles into practice:

- A commitment to relate sensitively to one another.
- A commitment to properly listen to and learn from people of other faith traditions.
- A commitment to see where we can work together to address common concerns, e.g. through the practice of community cohesion.
- A commitment to working together to challenge aspects of secular culture.
- A commitment within the overall process of dialogue to helping Christians to be more articulate about their faith – 1 Peter 3:15–16 – in this sense being clear and unapologetic for who we are and what we believe.

- A commitment to the whole Gospel – social, verbal and written.
- A commitment, especially where there is a majority culture of the other faith, to use words carefully.
- A commitment to the kind of listening, whereby the things on which we differ, hard issues of whatever kind, can be talked about in an atmosphere of trust. This means setting our engagement within the '*Missio Dei*', beginning with God and how as Christians we engage with people of other faiths when we come from a Trinitarian perspective.
- A commitment to a process which can be costly and sacrificial, but which, as one participant in 'The Listening Leader' project in Bradford expressed it: 'You are on holy ground when you are with a person of another faith; my listening and encounter has only served to strengthen my Christian faith'.[14]

In my own current context, I see this being played out effectively in a number of ways, though there is always more to learn. At the level of spiritual leadership in Greater Manchester, there is a quarterly meeting of Faith Community leaders, which involves the leaders of all the major Christian dominations, including the Black-led and Black majority churches, along with representatives from various Moslem, Jewish, Hindu and Sikh traditions. This network gives an opportunity for high quality listening, an expression of common concerns, and, where appropriate, speaking out with one voice. There is a commitment to understanding our differences and to wrestling with some of the implications of those differences.

An example of speaking with one voice was in connection with the launch of the 'Hope Not Hate' campaign in 2009, intended as a positive response to the campaigning for the European and local elections by extremist political parties such as the British National Party. The launch took place in

Manchester Cathedral, and involved all the faith community leaders, as well as representatives from the City Council, the Universities and many other people of good will. All signed a pledge of commitment.

In the area of the Diocese of Manchester where I have day to day responsibilities, I am involved in, and have been Chair of, the Bolton Faith Leaders Forum. This brings together nominated leaders from the three major faith communities in the area – Christian, Muslim and Hindu – along with members of the Interfaith Council, senior Council representatives and the Police. Our main aim, which can only be achieved by a serious commitment to listening, is to understand and speak into some of the areas of common concern within the communities where we live, and which together we are called to serve. Trust has thereby been built, such that if there is a particular incident that could exacerbate tensions between different communities, we are ready to listen to one another, and if appropriate issue a common statement for the benefit of the community as a whole. This was tested in a very particular way, and not found wanting, in the spring of 2010, in the light of the English Defence League's decision to hold an assembly in Bolton. Knowing that there were likely to be counter-demonstrations, and the potential of violence, we worked together not only to prevent damage to people, property and good relationships between the different communities, but together also launched the 'One Bolton' pledge which was subsequently signed by hundreds of people in the area. Such trust, however, also means that at other times a particular faith community will have something distinctive to say, and there is freedom to do that.

A further expression of this mutual commitment is expressed in the way that each of the three faith groups has the opportunity for a major public celebration of one of its festivals, with practical and financial support from the Council. As Christians, we chose Easter rather than Christmas as our opportunity, and, on a number of occasions now, on Holy

Saturday there has been a vibrant and creative celebration in the centre of the town, sharing the Easter message in words, music and drama with the crowds that gathered. Importantly, however, this also included the presence of and greetings from representatives of the Council of Mosques and the Hindu Forum. When it comes to their celebrations, I and other leaders have the opportunity of an equivalent role in their events.

To give another illustration, as a result of one particular parish priest's work in Bury, I have been regularly invited to a mosque in the town, for their Thursday evening prayers. I well remember my first visit, when after an hour and a half when the priest and I had sat at the back of the room where 100 or so men were offering their prayers, the leader of the mosque invited me, as 'our Bishop', to share something of my Christian journey and calling, and then to lead them in a prayer of blessing. This was followed by my shaking hands with all the men and boys present, and the hospitality of a shared meal. This was 'presence and engagement' in practice, and looking through the principles outlined above, many of the elements were certainly evident.

It was Thomas Merton's growing conviction that through encounters with people of other faiths we encounter God. For him it is too simplistic to say as Christians we are 'bringing the Gospel' to them; rather, we have an opportunity to meet Christ in 'the other':

> It is true that the visible church alone has the official mission to sanctify and teach all the nations. But no man knows that the stranger he meets coming out of the forest in a new country is not already an invisible member of Christ, and perhaps one who has some providential and prophetic message to utter.[15]

If to some this could sound like the proverbial 'watering down' of Christian distinctives, it is my conviction and experience that when we practise listening in this way, we can actually find ourselves and our faith renewed. When we truly listen to others whose beliefs and convictions differ from our own, and are not deflected by fears that as a result we shall somehow be 'tainted', we can only be enriched in our understanding of God and his purposes. Merton believed that for all Christians – but especially leaders – there would be no significant growth in faith and understanding without listening, and in relation to those from other faith communities, that was grounded in St Benedict's words: 'the divine presence is everywhere, and Christ is to be met in other people'.[16]

Listening for the leader therefore, in this and other contexts, is important not just because it enables truer communication and understanding, but because true listening and the openness it implies allows God to change, challenge and surprise us.

THE IMPLICATIONS OF INDABA FOR THE ECUMENICAL SCENE

It is my conviction that whatever areas of difference we have to address, the five 'ground rules of Indaba' are still relevant, along with the commitment to others outlined above, though obviously applied differently according to context. Before leaving this subject let me turn to the important area of relationships between Christians of different traditions. The bottom line of the ecumenical vocation in is in the words of our Lord in Chapter 17 of John's Gospel, a unity only possible when trust has been established by listening, and its outworking empowered and directed by the Holy Spirit:

'My prayer is not for them alone; I pray also for those who will believe in me through their message, that all of them may be one, Father, just as you are in me and I am in you. May they also be in us so that the world may believe that you have sent me.' (John 17:20–21, TNIV)

The 'Called to be One' statement from the World Council of Churches underlines earlier commitments from the member churches to the ultimate goal of 'full visible unity'. Understandings, however, continue to differ as to *how* Jesus' words in John 17 are to be interpreted. In essence, is 'being one' understood as something organic or institutional? Whatever the perspective, and the debate and the listening goes on, there is an understanding of the fundamental relationship between unity and mission – 'that the world might believe'. Unity reflects the Godhead, and witnesses to a broken and divided world; one of the reasons mission is impaired is because the 'world' does not see this unity of life and purpose.

The 2008 Lambeth Conference summed up its perspective and hopes in these words:

> Ecumenism is a meeting in truth, in Christ (Words of Pope John Paul II). It is part of the Church's vocation of reconciliation. The Church should be made up of reconcilers and reconciled, an instrument and sign of reconciliation. This role as a reconciling community is urgent because it offers a paradigm for what more generally humanity is seeking, in its search for authentic life, faith and truth. It should be pursued through servanthood, mutual support and most especially through prayer.[17]

I would want to add 'and through leaders learning to listen'! In practical terms I see this being enabled by:

- A commitment on the part of Church leaders in a locality to meet together for prayer, at which listening is at its heart, sharing common concerns and from that, devising appropriate strategies for ministry and mission in their area. This, coupled with a shared commitment to mission often seems to move things on further than simply studying reports and statements. (This was reflected in the theme for the 2010 Week of Prayer for Christian Unity: 'You are my witnesses'.)

- A commitment to the 'Lund principle' of 'not doing separately what we can do together'. This should include working to our respective strengths, and a sensible use of resources. One of the most exciting outworkings of this in recent years is the development of 'Fresh Expressions' of church, to which the Anglican, Methodist and United Reformed Churches are jointly committed.

- Although commitment to mission and social action is vital, and in some ways 'easier' than wrestling with theological and doctrinal issues, there should nevertheless be an ongoing commitment to a listening to each other and the recognition that we must not dodge the hard questions.

- A serious commitment to engaging with the 'new churches' that have emerged over the last 30 years, and a humility that allows us to discover what we can learn from one another that will strengthen our common witness. Linked to this is the recognition that denominational loyalty and allegiance is now largely only an issue for an older generation. Indeed many commentators would describe us as now being in a 'post-denominational culture'.

- In all this there should be a commitment to aiming for a depth of encounter as listening takes place, that will be personally transformative as well as thereby being a sign of hope to a fragmenting world.

The kind of listening that needs to be at the heart of these encounters will produce a longing, especially in the hearts of leaders, however far off the reality might be, to be in full union with other Christians, and that we hold the sense of pain until that is achieved.

LISTENING IS MINISTRY

Putting it quite simply, good listening, in whatever situation, but especially where there is significant difference, *is ministry*. We turn again to Jesus' own approach, and there see examples of this in so many encounters with people. To mention just three, despite so many differences between them, think of: his listening in the conversation with the Samaritan woman at the well, described in John 4; the dialogue we read between Jesus and the tax-collector Zaccheus, as described in Luke 19, as well as what we can only imagine went on behind closed doors, but had a life-transforming effect; and what happened with Simon the Pharisee, to whose house Jesus was invited for dinner, in Luke 7.

On the cross, in his dying moments, despite the physical, spiritual and emotional agony he was experiencing, Jesus was listening to the thief crucified alongside him. The one who had committed many wrongs cried out to the one who was sinless: 'Jesus, remember me when you come into your kingdom'. To which Jesus replied: 'Truly I tell you, today you will be with me in Paradise' (Luke 23:42–43).

Good listening is also *healing*. Cicely Saunders, founder of St Christopher's Hospice in Sydenham, Kent, and an inspiration to many others in what is now the world-wide Hospice Movement, once said: 'If someone is in a climate of listening, he or she will say things they wouldn't have said before'.

Where there is actual or potential difference, the leader helping to create such a climate offers a rare and precious gift.

The gift of being a good listener, a gift which requires constant practice, is perhaps the most healing gift anyone can possess; for it allows the other to be, enfolds them in a safe place, does not judge or advise them, accepts them as they are, without desiring to change them, and communicates support at a level deeper than words.[18]

Undoubtedly, such listening is also *costly*, whatever the context, in terms of time, attentiveness, and above all because of the commitment to self-discipline and concentration that is required. Furthermore, there are no guarantees of resolution where there is difference. But surely that is not a reason not to try, and after all we have not been left on our own in this task and process:

'I will not leave you orphaned; I am coming to you … the Advocate, the Holy Spirit whom the Father will send in my name, will teach you everything, and remind you of all that I have said to you.' (John 14:18, 26)

'And seriously trying means being seriously patient. Anyone who thinks that resolution can be reached in one leap without long mutual exploration, probing, challenge and clarification has not yet understood the nature of the riddle that the ironic fairy of history has posed for us in our time'.[19]

Even with the best kind of listening, we know that quick and easy solutions to serious issues of difference cannot always be found, though experience shows that personal growth and some progress is more likely when people feel genuinely heard and accepted, because barriers are lowered, and we become more generous. Being listened to helps us know more clearly what we are thinking, and why, and therefore to potentially take better actions as a result.

I suggest that these words from the third meeting of the Anglican Consultative Council in 1976, faced at that time with early debates on the ordination of women to the priesthood in the Anglican Communion, seem particularly apposite:

As in the first century, we can expect the Holy Spirit to *press us to listen to each other* (emphasis mine), to state new insights frankly, and to accept the implications of the Gospel new to us, whether painful or exhilarating.[20]

Chapter five

Creating a listening church

In this chapter, in the light of a God who still speaks today, we turn to the leader's role and responsibilities in helping to shape a better culture of listening in the local church.

As has already been acknowledged, the contemporary Church is having to navigate some choppy seas of uncertainty, as it seeks to discern how to operate in a rapidly changing culture. Addressing these realities is a vital part of the leader's role. The question is, how do we go about this? Once again, I would suggest that our first response ought to be to a commitment to listening – 'What is the Spirit saying to the church?' Leaders are rightly concerned to see their churches grow, to develop new strategies for changing times, to have appropriate structures in place and to try and stem the decline in influence as well as numbers, which churches of many denominations are experiencing, and to serve the communities where they are set more effectively. This can result in what looks and feels like anxiety-driven activity. Stopping to listen, individually and with others, for what God might be saying for their situation would be so much better for the leader and those for whom they are responsible.

A serious commitment to listening could also enable one of the most important tasks for the leader at times of transition, namely to discern what should be taken into the future and what ought to be left behind. It is about:

Letting the shape of the church be re-configured around the new realities God is presenting to us, rather than the realities to which we tried to be faithful in a previous age.[1]

There is both a sense of excitement and stress for many leaders, seeking to appropriately re-imagine the Church for tomorrow while still ministering in the ever-demanding Church of today.

> A clergy leader is a liminal figure, living in the border-land between the church and the world, the present and the future, inherited church and emerging church.[2]

Along with others who have written on this subject, I applaud so many of the new initiatives that are being taken to re-think and re-imagine how the Church should be for the twenty-first century. Indeed, in my own ministry as a local church leader I have been involved in pioneering new initiatives, and now at a regional level am committed to setting up and supporting new ways of church being expressed. However, after nearly forty years of ordained ministry in the Church of England, I have seen many initiatives come and go. It concerns me that in a desperate attempt to turn things around, churches and their leaders will quite often unquestioningly 'latch on to' one of the latest initiatives or ideas that have 'worked' somewhere else in the country or world. *This* might be the 'magic bullet' that will bring renewal and growth, or be the panacea for the disappointments they are facing and the challenges they are experiencing locally.

Some of these initiatives have come from the 'centre', such as the 1990's Decade of Evangelism, which largely had its origins in the 1988 Lambeth Conference of Anglican Bish-ops, but was also taken up by several of the other major denominations. Others have come more from the 'edges', whether 'Mission England' with Billy Graham in the 1980s, or various so-called 'outpourings' of the Holy Spirit, from the Kansas City prophets and 'Toronto' in the 1990s, via Pensa-cola and Florida in the early part of the twenty-first century. The 1990s also saw the 'Alpha' course begin to grow from its beginnings at Holy Trinity Brompton in London into a world-wide phenomenon now, embraced by most of the major Christian denominations, including Roman Catholic and Orthodox.

For the leader seeking to 'listen to what the Spirit is saying to the Church', at any given moment in its local and global history, it can be hard to discern what is the latest 'fad' which might soon be dead in the water, and what truly is a fresh move of the Holy Spirit. In my 'ministerial lifetime', there have been 'prophecies' of revival, clearly exaggerated and manifestly unfulfilled, that have left leaders and congregations alike at best confused, and at worst cynical. Bishop Gavin Reid, formerly Director of Mission England, and later Bishop of Maidstone, once said to me: 'I'm wary of hitching myself to every bandwagon that comes by, but equally I don't want to miss the one that God might actually be on!'

We need to heed Ian Stackhouse's wise words: 'Ministry is far less to do with innovation and initiative than it is to do with listening and attentiveness'.[3]

Creating a listening church starts with the leader's own commitment to that three-fold listening – to God, the world and the Church.

Once again it was Dietrich Bonhoeffer, writing in the dark days of his imprisonment by the Nazis in World War Two, who looked with characteristic prophetic insight to a time in the future when he hoped there would be:

> A return to the roots of our being, in order that out of silence, prayer and hope, we might once more receive from God new words and a new way of stating not our message but his.[4]

Thomas Merton himself argued that without a serious commitment to listening:

> we cannot see what we do ... we cannot understand the significance of the world in which we must act ... we

remain small, limited, divided, partial; we adhere to the insufficient, permanently united to our narrow group and interests, losing sight of justice and charity, seized by the passions of the moment, and finally we betray Christ.[5]

As we know, mission is often portrayed simply in terms of 'action'. What Merton is saying here is that action must be married with reflection on the part of the leader and the church. Both the Bible and the wisdom of leaders down the centuries of Christian history demonstrate clearly that a commitment to disciplined listening is the wellspring for fruitful action.

If action is out of touch with an interior source of prayer it eventually becomes arid and barren, and we find ourselves the victims of busyness, frenetic over-activity. But conversely, if our prayer becomes cut off from action, it is cut off from life. Here is the equilibrium of contemplation and action.[6]

Or, as David Runcorn has expressed it in a more recent publication: 'The outer life of the Church must always be lived in careful partnership with its hidden vocation'.[7]

Making listening and reflection a priority is not about being inwardly focused when we need to be getting on with the business of equipping people for mission and more effective Christian living. Nor is it adopting a spirituality suited only to quieter, more contemplative personality types. It is about being willing to go deeper with God, in order to see more clearly what he is wanting to say and do. It is a means by which we ensure we avoid being task-driven and purely pragmatic, so that what is offered through the Church is a way of living as God would want us to: in his world, but walking to a different drumbeat.

To quote Runcorn again:

> True contemplation nurtures an attentive heart that can discern God's love and presence in all of life. It is as much about radical engagement with the world as it is about disciplined withdrawal and stillness. Each needs the other.[8]

Being attentive is about learning to be authentically present to ourselves, others and the world in the greater context of God's love and purposes. It can renew our capacity to be more expectant to see God at work, in itself a healthy antidote to the cynicism that can so easily beset the leader. Making space to listen helps put into better perspective some of the anxieties and inadequacies the leader can experience. Here then is no escapism, but an approach to the task of leadership that enables a truer understanding of the real and often messy contexts in which life is lived and leadership expressed. Listening is the cradle where contemplation of God and the world can meet. It can help us discern what steps of action and prophetic witness to take in order to enable transformation of the lives of individuals and communities. Thus a church being shaped for effective mission will have at its heart a leadership 'setting the tone' for listening. It will offer, to its members and to the community it serves, opportunities for silence, space and reflection. It will seek to develop the congregation's understanding of the importance of the inseparable link between contemplation and action.

Thus the best starting point for mission and engagement in a parish might be to run a weekend, or even a week of guided prayer. Surprising prophetic action, based on God's priorities and thereby grounded in a healthy detachment from anxiety about results and success, could follow from this. Times such as this can help a church to establish – simply but profoundly – a reflective, silent oasis where Christian and 'seeker' alike can discover greater depth in themselves and God, and thereby a better way of living.

THE LEADER'S ROLE IN DISCERNMENT

I have already used certain words that are integral to the leader's role in developing a 'listening church'. Among these are two in particular that must be looked at in more detail – *discernment* and *prophecy/the prophetic*. I begin with a brief look at their use and meaning in the Bible.

Both words, in my experience, can be used very loosely. For example a church in a period of interregnum or vacancy might put together a profile for their new leader, specifying someone 'who can speak prophetically and has the gift of discernment'. It sounds good and difficult to argue with, but what is actually meant and understood by these words?

The nature of prophecy as referred to in the Scriptures has been much debated among biblical scholars. I take an overall definition of prophecy as being 'the declaring of God's will to his people'. In the early Church, Origen defined prophecy as 'meaningful knowledge of unseen things through speech' which is taught to others. The one with a prophetic gift, therefore, is offering a supernatural word of revelation, which St Paul regarded as the most important gift for the church's life as a community:

> Follow the way of love and eagerly desire spiritual gifts, especially the gift of prophecy ... I would like every one of you to speak in tongues, but I would rather have you prophesy. (1 Cor. 14:1, 5)

From the New Testament (though there is the example of Agabus in Acts 11:28) it is clear that prophecy is not only about disclosing future events – the main emphasis of the Old Testament prophets – but can also address contemporary situations, in such a way as to bring encouragement and comfort (1 Cor. 14:3), challenge (1 Cor. 14:25) and also can include a call to repentance (Rev. 11:3).

Canon Professor Anthony Thiselton helpfully concludes:

> Prophecy combines pastoral insights into the needs of persons, communities and situations with the ability to address these with a God-given utterance or longer discourse (whether unprompted or prepared with judgement, decision and rational reflection) leading to challenge or comfort, judgement or consolation, but ultimately building up the addressees.[9]

'Discernment of the Spirits' (*diakriesis pneumaton*), another of the varied gifts that Paul describes in 1 Cor. 12–14, is clearly understood to be closely related to prophecy, since the prophetic always needs checks. This is clear from examples in both the Old and New Testaments. In the Old Testament, where the presenting problem at a particular point in Israel's history was the worship of other gods, we read:

> 'If a prophet, or one who foretells by dreams, appears among you and announces to you a miraculous sign or wonder, and if the sign or wonder of which he has spoken takes place, and he says "Let us follow other gods" (gods you have not known) "and let us worship them", you must not listen to the words of that prophet or dreamer. The Lord your God is testing you to find out whether you love him with all your heart and with all your soul.' (Deut. 13:1–3)

From the ministry of Jesus, we find these words recorded in Matthew 24:24–25:

> 'For false Christs and false prophets will appear and perform great signs and miracles to deceive even the elect – if that were possible. See I have told you ahead of time.'

Or from the First Letter to the Thessalonians:

> Do not put out the Spirit's fire; do not treat prophecies
> with contempt. Test everything. Hold on to the good.
> Avoid every kind of evil. (1 Thess. 5:19–21)

Professor James Dunn identifies discernment as 'an evaluation, an investigation, a weighing of the prophetic utter-
ance'[10]. It is in essence to do with the difference between
identifying communications that come from God and those
which don't.

The verb form *diakrinein* appears later, in 1 Corinthians
14:29, in connection with weighing what a 'prophet' has said.
R. Collins connects it to discerning true prophecy from
false.[11] This gift enables the church to ascertain whether
someone is preaching 'another gospel' (Gal. 1:6) or 'another
Jesus' (2 Cor. 11:4), but with the Corinthian enthusiasm 'for
spirits' (1 Cor. 14:12) – that is the manifestations of the Spirit
– discernment of all kinds is necessary.

'Discernment' brings out the mutual interdependence of
the other 'speaking' gifts Paul refers to in 1 Corinthians. This
is why it is especially important for those in leadership to
seek this gift. According to Paul, prophecy is the most valuable gift for building up the Church and speaking to the
world, but it always requires testing and evaluation. (I will
give some practical examples of how this might work out
later in the chapter.)

Back in the late 1970s, Michael Harper wrote a book on
leadership, *Let My People Grow*, which was very influential
for many church leaders of my generation. He tried then to
alert the Church to the importance of listening in order to be
truly prophetic:

> … the Church and the world miss something vital when
> the voice of the prophet is no longer heard in the land.
> We are living in days which are not exactly calculated to

encourage the career of a prophet … his main function is to 'listen'. *The Church today is notoriously bad at listening and being still and quiet enough to do so* (italics mine).[12]

This makes clear that listening, in order that the prophetic may be spoken, and its significance discerned, is not just for the benefit of the 'in house' life of the church, but for the sake of the world. Sadly, one reaction to Paul's teaching on spiritual gifts is to dismiss them as irrelevant for today's Church. Equally, it is all too easy for those who have embraced them, to seek to 'domesticate' those gifts, or to be naive about their meaning and application. Part of the leader's task, therefore, is not just to encourage a listening to God for insights he may want to give the church, but to remind the members that the Church is a sacrament of the Kingdom. If that kingdom's influence is to grow, which is God's intention, then it needs prophetic insights, given through the church, understanding itself to be an instrument of transformation, in the lives of both individuals and communities.

Part of the role of the leader who listens is to be in touch with the voices and values that are shaping the community the church serves, and also those who may be voice-less. Local issues might be concerns about housing, unemployment, violent crime, racial tensions, or the environment. To 'speak into' these matters, to engage in the 'prophetic' understood like this, can be costly, particularly if it involves taking a stand against injustice or ethically dubious practices. That is certainly how it was for many in the Old Testament prophetic tradition, as the prophets sought, depending on the situation, to challenge injustice among God's people, or to speak a word of compassion to those facing oppression of any kind.

In an earlier chapter I referred to being part of a campaign launched in Manchester Cathedral called 'Hope Not Hate'. This was a coalition of leaders of many different faiths and others of good will in the community, concerned to offer another voice in contrast to the potentially divisive not to say racist policies being promoted by extreme nationalist parties. All of us involved subsequently received hate mail and criticism, largely from those who subscribed to those extremist views, but, it has to be said, also from within the churches. Similarly, in the light of the growth of extremist parties, when I wrote to the local press on behalf of the Christians in the Bolton area, encouraging people to use their democratic vote in European, local and national elections, while many were supportive, again there were those in the churches as well as the wider community who said 'bishops shouldn't meddle in politics!'

John Pritchard puts it well when he says:

> Theologically, the priest is having to make the distinction between discerning God's presence in blessing or judgement ... The prophetic task is to look into the depth of events and discern their direction, either towards God's kingdom or subtly deviating from it.[13]

Thus, true mission always has about it a prophetic dimension: a calling to speak out against what is wrong and unjust. But it also includes a call to discern, recognise and announce the presence of God in the world.

I have come to understand the importance of recognising and celebrating diversity in the discernment process. A true understanding of discernment is never a 'one size fits all'. It should be possible for every culture to learn to discern its own priorities and patterns for walking to God's drumbeat in their particular context. Thus, Christians in Turkey, a 'secular Moslem' country, will need to learn to discern what their priorities should be, and how they should live, in a way that will be radically different from their sisters and brothers in the Congo. Russian Baptists will need their leaders to help them see how to live out the Gospel, in ways that will be different from the Coptic Orthodox Church in Egypt. Anglicans in Pakistan, where in fact all the different denominations of Christians make up less than 2 per cent of the population, will discern priorities in ways that differ from Anglicans in Australia. To bring it closer to home, churches in Dorset, where I spent my teenage years, or Cumbria, where I once served as Diocesan Missioner, have a very different context in which to work out their ministry and mission from churches in Greater Manchester and Rossendale, where I currently live and work.

I believe that when it comes to local issues, the Church's life and witness is strengthened by celebrating a vibrant diversity, connecting appropriately to its local context, which, as I hope I have made clear earlier, does not mean 'anything goes'.

Again within the Church of England, one way that is made clear is reflected in that wording of the Preface prior to the Oaths and Declarations to which I referred in the previous chapter. I quote again:

The Church of England is part of the One, Holy, Catholic and Apostolic Church, worshipping the one true God, Father, Son and Holy Spirit. It professes the faith uniquely revealed in the Holy Scriptures and set forth in the catholic creeds, which faith the Church is called upon to proclaim afresh in each generation. Led by the Holy Spirit, it has borne witness to Christian truth in its historic formularies, the Thirty-nine articles of religion, the Book of Common Prayer and the Ordering of Bishops, Priests and Deacons.

In the declaration you are about to make, will you affirm your loyalty to this inheritance of faith as your inspiration and guidance under God in bringing the grace and truth of Christ to this generation and making Him known to those in your care?

The importance of the 'inheritance of faith' is clear, but this does not preclude the Spirit leading God's people to different priorities locally, or how church should be expressed, according to the contexts in which they find themselves, as a result of either particular opportunities or pressure points.

The need for a healthier understanding of variety and diversity as to how God speaks is further underlined in the ways in which different denominations and Christian traditions expect to 'hear' God speak. So, for example, within the Pentecostal/Charismatic 'stream', there will be an expectation, especially when people come together for worship, that certain spiritual gifts as described particularly by Paul in his letters will be in evidence: tongues, interpretation, words of prophecy, knowledge and wisdom. There might be a sharing of dreams, visions, pictures and other revelations through which it is believed God may be speaking. For 'classic' Evangelicals, the Bible is all – the supreme authority in all matters of faith and conduct. The Bible is the word of God; it is uniquely inspired by the Holy Spirit, who enables the words on the pages to live for the individual, and calls those in leadership to faithfully teach and preach that word. For those within the Catholic or Orthodox traditions, it is often primarily through sacrament and symbol that God is encountered; his 'otherness' is celebrated. A call to 'worship the Lord in the beauty of holiness; let the whole earth stand in awe of him'. In common with all streams is Scripture being seen as the touchstone against which everything must be tested.

I am aware here of the danger here of laying myself open to the charge of gross over-simplification and generalisation! My point, however, is that down the centuries churches and their leaders, rather than celebrating – in those words of the writer to the Hebrews – the 'many and various ways' in which God speaks, have implicitly or explicitly suggested that God speaks only '*this way*'. This has led to criticism and misunderstanding, and has also meant that the people of God have missed out on that rich variety of ways in which God has spoken, and goes on speaking. Thankfully there has been significant movement in recent decades to break down some of this polarisation. However, leaders can still sometimes be afraid to move out of their own 'comfort zones' and the traditions that have shaped them, for fear of being somehow 'contaminated' by something alien. They can also be reluctant to expose others to insights from unfamiliar sources.

I carry a powerful memory from my time as Warden of the Lee Abbey Community in North Devon. I was speaking at a weekend that drew together four churches from different parts of the United Kingdom: an Anglican parish church, a Vineyard church, members of a Methodist circuit and a charismatic Baptist Church from Wales, planted by American Southern Baptists. I have to say I approached my task with some trepidation! In particular, knowing their different approaches to worship and ways of 'hearing' God, how could we best enable an openness to, and authentic encounter with, God? I will never forget on the Sunday morning, walking into the Octagonal Lounge, where worship and teaching takes place at Lee Abbey. I realised that our Music Director was rehearsing a Russian Orthodox Trisagion to be used later in the Holy Communion Service. I watched and listened as people from all those four very diverse Christian communities sang beautifully, and more importantly were deeply moved by the whole experience. What in advance might have seemed to many of them at best unfamiliar and at worst alien and inappropriate, became a means of true worship even in rehearsal.

The service was led, in a relaxed but reverent way, by one of my chaplain colleagues, according to the Church of England's Common Worship Order. Reflecting with the different church groups after the service, I heard some interesting responses. The Anglicans who had not previously experienced 'words of knowledge' being shared heard some insights they needed to take note of as a church. Eyes were opened to liturgy as 'freedom in a framework', rather than simply being about going through words on a page. The Methodists spoke of wanting to introduce prayer ministry into their services, because that had been a 'natural' part of the Communion service they had experienced. Individuals spoke of having felt 'touched' by God; some of their leaders had been prayed for and as a result sensed a fresh equipping from God for their ministries. From the two other churches – for whom 'liturgy' had been, as one put it, a 'red rag to a bull', something that was predictable and 'quenched the Spirit' – there was a new awareness of the richness of the words and tradition that lay behind them. As another person put it, they had 'heard' God speak through the liturgy, and recognised that though their tradition had no written liturgy, in fact they recognised that they actually had a very predictable pattern as to what happened in their worship. And all that in less than forty-eight hours!

The 'many and various' theme carries through to the ways in which some of the most influential Church leaders from different eras and spiritual traditions have spoken of their experience of 'hearing' God. The Quaker, George Fox, wrote and spoke about the Lord 'opening a truth' to him, by which he meant that God had spoken in some way, though not audibly. John Calvin wrote of the 'inner testimony of the Holy Spirit' in his life and ministry. St Ignatius referred to what he called 'movements of the soul', referring to feelings and desires that could be gifts given directly by God to move the individual closer to him, or to some appropriate course of action. The language used might be different, but in each instance for these and other leaders who were serious about hearing God not only for themselves but for the church, there was a commitment to 'practise the presence of God', and to be what the author John Ortberg has called 'relentlessly responsive'.

GETTING PRACTICAL

Given an understanding and acceptance of these principles, how might the leader go about creating a culture of listening in the church or churches for which they have responsibility?

The Leader Sets the Tone

Firstly, and without apology, I repeat that this has to begin in the leader's own life and priorities. For some, grasping the importance of listening has meant ensuring putting aside in the diary each month a half day or a whole day that is clear of any other commitments. Those who have taken such a step say that each time it comes around, there can be 101 seemingly pressing reasons why 'I haven't got time'. But equally they would say that, having embarked on this discipline, not only is their own relationship with God enriched and renewed, but they become more open to the promptings of the Holy Spirit and gain fresh perspectives for their ministerial responsibilities. It is about 'discovering God's voice amongst the other voices inside and outside ourselves'.[14]

Making this commitment means moving from a mindset that says 'I can't afford the time', to 'I can't afford not to make the time'. My own experience, in the different parishes and places where I have exercised leadership, is that when I have communicated to others that this is my practice and intention, people are by and large very supportive as they realise the church is likely to benefit from the leader 'stepping aside' in this way. Also I believe it helps to model something important to church members about the importance of rhythm in our lives.

Listening for the 'Sounds of God' in Worship

Secondly, I believe it is a leadership responsibility to help people learn both to use silence and, linked to that, to learn to listen for and respond to God's promptings in the context of worship. For a congregation not used to this, the best starting point for this may be in the context of a small group. If this is something new, the leader needs to have realistic expectations!

Ways of helping people to use space and silence in a small group might include:

- Getting the members to bring a verse of Scripture, leave some silence, and then turn it into a meditation prayer.

- Spending a period of time in silence looking at a meaningful painting or icon, and inviting people to write down what they think God is saying to them as individuals, or to the church for its ministry and mission. In due course, they can be encouraged to share what they have written down, with others listening without initial comment. Then, after a few moments, have a time of shared reflection as to the significance of what has been offered.

- Starting with some quiet reflective music being played, the group can be invited to spend time in quiet, intentionally listening for what God might be wanting to say. Then the leader can invite individuals to share what they *think* God might be saying – even if they are not at all sure – especially words of encouragement for another member, by giving them the 'word' as a gift from God. Learning to grow in confidence in the small group can then mean people are more confident to share insights in a larger setting, as well as taking opportunities in their day to day lives. (I say this to ensure, as I indicated earlier, that we don't wrongly 'domesticate' spiritual gifts and insights.)

Especially if this is new to people, it is important that a 'de-briefing' time happens, when members of the group can reflect on the experience and the leader can seek to interpret what is going on.

In an earlier chapter, I quoted E. M. Forster's words about 'poor talkative little Christianity'. It is in the context of public worship and larger numbers, whatever the style and approach, that these words most apply. Whether we use written liturgy or not, we are far too talkative. I have been as guilty as anyone! I have often suggested after the sermon, or after some sung worship, that we keep a few moments of silence ... but then found I'm moving things on after one or two minutes, and the congregation are beginning, more or less subtly, to look at their watches! Again, it is a leadership responsibility to set the tone on this. We must teach and model the place of silence being valuable in itself, and also that out of silence might come a prophetic word or some other kind of spiritual insight that individuals or the congregation as a whole need to hear. I have already quoted George Fox, and our Quaker friends have much to teach us here. It is not silence for its own sake that is being sought, but what they describe as a 'living stillness'.

It has been my practice in the different churches I have led to invite any who wished to come early before the service, and be part of a group praying for all who will be involved in the worship. I have encouraged people to spend part of the time in silence. Time and time again, significant words of Scripture or other spiritual insights have been highlighted which have been shared later in the service, often having a powerful effect on individuals or the church and its calling.

Listening can Transform Meetings

Thirdly, I am convinced that our church meetings – especially business ones – could be transformed as experiences in themselves, as well as their overall effectiveness, by more time spent listening to God and one another.

People arriving at meetings have often spent busy and demanding days out at work or in the home. Some kind of

'Gathering Liturgy', rather than what I call a brief 'nod to God' could make all the difference to how they address the business of the meeting. One way to do this – and there are endless variations – is to begin by offering the meeting and time spent together to God. Then, either in the group as a whole, or in twos and threes, each person is offered two minutes to respond to questions such as: 'How are you feeling tonight?', 'What kind of day have you had?' and 'What has gone well, and what has been difficult?' After this sharing and listening to one another, there can be a time of silence in which we hold what has been shared before God, some reading of the Scriptures and other appropriate prayer, following which the meeting is ready to share its business and get on with its tasks in a new spirit.

If this is new for the leader and those who are involved in the meeting, there may be both inward and outward battles to be overcome, to do with the vulnerability that comes from sharing and listening. There may also be a more practical anxiety that this 'Gathering Liturgy', added to an already overfull agenda, will mean an even later night home! Let me say that, whenever I have approached meetings in this way, it has rarely made the meeting longer; indeed, we have often finished earlier, and looked with amazement at one another as to how we had got through so much in the time. The point is: there has been an opportunity to be truly present to each other and to God. This is vital if we are to discern his priorities for the work he is calling the church to do – we are learning to work to his agenda, which may be different from ours.

Sometimes in the course of a meeting, when there is lack of clarity about an issue or decision, and even more when there is conflict, part of the leader's role is to call people to silence, to take time to reflect. This is not about masking problems, but in order to regain perspective, to let people calm down and, if necessary, 're-wind', so as to come at whatever the issue is in a fresh way.

It has also been my practice to encourage church councils, or other leadership groups and teams, to have a regular (at least annual) day or weekend away. Not only does this give more space, especially to deal with some of the 'bigger' issues more adequately, but part of the day can and should be given over to listening. Sometimes I have done this as a corporate exercise, and at others sent people off to begin by reflecting individually in silence. On one occasion, for example, I asked church council members to reflect on what they thought the three main priorities of the church should be in the coming year. Having come back together, we then discussed what people's thoughts were. By the end of the day we were unanimous on what those three should be. During the following year, at each of our subsequent meetings, each member of the church council was part of a smaller group that looked at and worked on one or other of those areas. The energy people brought to the table as a result of this listening process meant that significant progress was made, which might not have happened had the earlier listening process not taken place.

I find these words of Thomas Kelly helpful in this regard:

> There is a way of ordering our mental life on more than one level at once. On one level we may be thinking, discussing, seeing, calculating, meeting all the demands of external affairs. But deep within, behind the scenes, at a profounder level, we may also be in prayer ... and a gentle receptiveness to divine breathings.[15]

LOOK, LISTEN AND ACT

Once a church has begun to take listening to God and one another more seriously, and people begin to understand the importance of discerning his vision and priorities, one of the most helpful tools I have found to develop this is the 'Mission Audit' process. For whatever reason this resource, which was used to great effect by many churches in the 1980s and 1990s, seems to have rather gone out of fashion in recent years. (Of course there have been other developments, such as the work done by Robert Warren around 'Growing Healthy Churches', and local initiatives helping churches to develop 'Mission Action Plans').

For those unfamiliar with it, Mission Audit is a technical term for what is actually a very straightforward, but often neglected process. Essentially, it is about seeing how you can 'take the temperature' of the local church, see its setting within the local community and thereby assess its effectiveness under God. Its history as a term goes back to the early 1980s, when the Church of England asked twelve Christians from overseas to look and listen, and then say what they thought about the church. There were a number of positive reflections, but also significant criticisms. In particular, they said that Anglican churches in England did not think carefully enough about what they were doing, and so lacked vision and direction. They suggested that there should be a 'Mission Audit produced for use by all parochial church councils which would enable them to examine the work of their church and community, and plan for the future'.

As a result, resources were produced to help in this process, both by the Church of England, and some of the other major denominations. At its heart, Mission Audit tries to find out the facts about the present, so that a clearer picture about the future can emerge. The focus on *mission* means:

- Looking outwards as well as inwards.
- Being committed to seeing God's kingdom extended.
- Taking the needs of the community seriously.
- Helping church members to see their ministry as being at work and home, as well as in the church.

Although the word '*audit*' is usually associated with finance, the Latin root of the word demonstrates what it is actually about:

- A commitment to listening.
- Trying to hear what as many people in the church and the community are really saying.
- Above all, trying to hear through all this what God is saying.

As I indicated above, we are talking about an essentially straightforward process, by means of which, a church can *stop, look, listen* and then *act*. Many of our churches are very active, running events which can be both enjoyable and effective. But there is a need from time to time for all churches – even the most successful – to stop and think why they are doing these things. Even if they were God's priorities in the past, are they now? 'It is not enough to be busy; the question is, "What are we busy about?"' (Henry David Thoreau).

Listening both to God, and to what people are saying – not just the words, but how they are saying them and why they are saying them – are both crucial. The aim of a Mission Audit is, with God's guidance, to help produce a more healthy church. This means that once there has been careful reflection and appropriate consultation, a key role of the leader is to begin to paint a vision of the future: a vision that opens people's eyes, that helps people to dream dreams, but which is also 'earthed' through decisions which are made.

Audits are essentially of two kinds: general and limited. A general audit looks at the whole life and work of the church and its ministry and mission to the community in which it is set. A limited audit will look at only one or two parts of the life of the church or community. Three years into the parish where I was a vicar in Bradford in the 1990s, we embarked on a general audit. We didn't use the audit word, but called it our 'Vision and Commitment' process. Through wide consultation and the involvement of people of all ages, we were trying to discern what God's vision for the church was for the coming years, and what kind of commitment would we need to make to be faithful to it. This took place over a six-month period, and it was about a year after we started that I shared with the congregation as a whole what we sensed our priorities needed to be, which in turn led to some quite radical decisions being made, both affecting our internal life as well as our mission and outreach. At other times, we looked at a specific area of the life of the church, for example, our work with children and young people, and how that might need to change and develop.

As a rule, if there is a need for fresh vision and you want to know where God is leading you, then, by whatever means and using whatever resources are helpful, embark on a general audit. If the overall vision and direction is clear, but you are aware that some areas of church life are 'creaking', then a limited audit would be the best approach.

For me, the insights in John Finney's book, *The Well Church Book*, have been extremely helpful in all that I have outlined above, not least rooting the concept in what he refers to as the first mission audits – those of the Seven Churches of Asia, as described in Revelation Chapters 2 and 3. Summarising what he has to say:

Audits are especially for leaders, who have to do something about the suggestions made.

An audit is about trying to hear what God is saying.

Audits have to be based on known facts, not fantasy.

Be prepared for the pain of audit. Truth can hurt.

An audit should tell you what is right about the church, as well as what is wrong.

An audit which does not point people to God is merely an exercise in management. It will produce an earth-bound church which does not have that 'touch of heaven'.

It is no use beginning an audit unless the church is prepared to study the results and act on it: 'He who has an ear, let him *hear* what the Spirit says'.[16]

Ultimately, only God can create a responsive listening church, but he needs our co-operation, and leaders setting the tone. To do so can be risky and at times unnerving, but again to quote John Finney:

Stepping as a church into 'pilgrim faith' is what it's all about: a journey of discovery into what it means to be God's people, God's Church.[17]

Afterword – The Lord who listens

Of all the skills of leadership, listening is the most valuable – and least understood. Most captains of industry listen only sometimes, and then only to other leaders. But a few, the great ones, never stop listening. That's how they become aware before anyone else of unseen problems and opportunities.[1]

In the preceding chapters, our focus has been on the call and challenge for leaders to learn to listen for the 'sounds of God', and the many, various and sometimes surprising ways in which he speaks, as well as some of the things that can get in the way of true listening. But all listening begins and ends in God, and the Lord who speaks is also the Lord who listens. As one of the Anglican collects puts it, he is 'always more ready to hear than we are to pray'.

Anne Long reminds us that this is of course at the very heart of his nature, because:

He is not one but three, a Trinity of Father, Son and Holy Spirit. Rublev's fifteenth-century icon of the Trinity depicts three angels looking at each other in mutual listening, loving and self giving, three yet one in unity and purpose. It reminds us of the ceaseless communication that is going on within the Godhead.[2]

EXPECTING THAT GOD WILL LISTEN

Although the experience of people within the pages of Scripture is sometimes like ours – a feeling that, having prayed, heaven is silent, or any response seems slow in coming – none the less there is a motif running throughout that God *is* one who listens to his people. For example, after many years of oppression in Egypt, with the Israelites 'groaning under their slavery', we read that 'their cry for help rose up to God'. He heard their groaning, remembered the Covenant he had made with their ancestors, the Patriarchs Abraham, Isaac and Jacob, and 'God took notice of them' (Exod. 2:25).

We also find within the pages of the Old Testament numerous examples of the phrase 'Hear my prayer' being used, especially in the Psalms. The following are just a few examples:

'Hear my prayer, O Lord,
And give ear to my cry;
Do not hold your peace at my tears.' (Ps. 39:12)

Hear my prayer, O God;
Give ear to the words of my mouth. (Ps. 54:2)

O Lord God of hosts,
Hear my prayer;
Give ear O God of Jacob. (Ps. 84:8)

The theme of waiting for God to respond to his prayer, expounded in Psalm 37, has its painful application in Psalms 38 and 39, but then leads to a positive outcome for King David as expressed in Psalm 40. In his prayer of thanksgiving for deliverance – whether that was from sickness, sin or danger – he begins:

I waited patiently for the Lord;
He inclined to me and *heard* my cry. (Ps. 40:1)

This expectation that God will listen to our prayers and indeed our cries is, of course, reflected in the liturgical responses found in many of our churches:

'Lord in your mercy: hear our prayer'
'O Lord hear our prayer: and let our cry come unto you.'

In the course of King Solomon's prayer when the Temple was dedicated, we find him also linking these themes of 'hearing' and God's mercy:

> 'Hear the plea of your servant and of your people Israel when they pray towards this place; May you hear from heaven your dwelling place; hear and forgive.' (2 Chr. 6:21)

At several points in his life and leadership, the prophet Jeremiah finds himself at the end of his tether as a result of the lack of responsiveness and opposition to the message God had called him to bring. On one occasion, having gone as far as to curse the day he was born and complained bitterly to God, he found, I imagine to his surprise, that, far from this distancing him further from his relationship with God, he is both heard and reassured:

> 'And I will make you to this people
> A fortified wall of bronze;
> They will fight against you,
> But they shall not prevail over you,
> For I am with you, to save and deliver you
> Says the Lord.' (Jer. 15:20)

THE LISTENING OF JESUS

The journey to becoming an effective leader begins, as the rule of Benedict puts it, with 'obedient listening'.

It seems, from the Gospel accounts, that Jesus lived his life in daily awareness, first, that he was one who was 'dearly loved', and, second, out of that sense of unconditional love and acceptance believed that his Father would listen to him.

This was the foundation on which he built his life and ministry, which is what in turn enabled him to be able to listen well, and bring healing, hope, forgiveness and challenge to those who he was called to lead and serve.

As we have noted earlier in the book, this was also why it was always a priority for Jesus to set aside time to pray, with the expectation that he would be heard:

> Now during those days he went out to the mountain to pray, and he spent the night in prayer to God. (Luke 6:12)

It seems that even in the agony he experienced in Gethsemane, though he had not received the answer that in his humanity he might have wanted, none the less Luke records that Jesus experienced a strengthening presence, and in that sense knew he had been heard:

> He withdrew from them about a stone's throw, knelt down and prayed, 'Father if you are willing, remove this cup from me, yet, not my will but yours be done.' Then an angel from heaven appeared to him and gave him strength. In his anguish he prayed more earnestly and his sweat became like great drops of blood falling down on the ground. (Luke 22:43–44)

Having observed earlier the way in which Jesus modelled the 'listening heart' of his Father, I end with two, out of many examples in the Gospels, of how that quality of and commitment to listening led to healing and wholeness for individuals. I invite you to take time to reflect on what will be to most readers very familiar examples, in order both to further inspire and encourage your own listening, as well as perhaps to lead you to further reflection on the many other examples and incidents in Jesus' life and ministry, from which we as leaders can learn.

THE WOMAN WITH THE HAEMORRHAGE: MARK 5:25–34

One of Mark's literary strategems is the device of fitting one story inside another and interrelating them. His main purpose seems to be to set side by side two or more comparable elements, or contrasting attitudes. Here, it is between Jairus, the male, respected, synagogue leader, whose daughter was at the point of death, and a woman who had suffered from bleeding for twelve years, causing her not only to be physically in need but also seen as ritually unclean. Furthermore she was penniless as a result of spending her money on trying to find a cure for her illness.

Jesus set off, along with a large crowd 'pressing in on him', for Jairus' house (verse 24), and it is in this context that the second story is told. Her ritual uncleanness (see Leviticus 15:25–30) may account in part for the woman's somewhat furtive approach (verse 27) coming up behind him. The touching of the garment would have been related to a common belief at the time that the clothing carried the power of the person (see Acts 19:12).

Her place in the narrative at this point harmonises with that of the synagogue official. For all their differences of sex, status and public recognition, she too has perceived on the basis of reports she had 'heard about Jesus' (verse 27) that he will be able to meet what she sees as her basic need, physically and ritually. In this situation, where there was no speaking of need on her part in literal words, what do we learn from the 'listening of Jesus'?

- Her touch achieved what she had hoped for (verse 28–29), but she had not allowed for the cost to Jesus himself: 'Jesus realised that power had gone out from him' (verse 30).
- He 'knew' this without words being spoken.

- Despite the pressures to get to the sick girl's house, he was able to 'hear' and respond to the need of the woman.
- He took time to stop and respond to the woman's faith. 'Daughter, your faith has made you well: go in peace and be healed of your disease' (verse 34). Her commitment was complete. She had received power already (verse 29); in these words of Jesus she heard and received peace (verse 34). And the clue is her faith (verse 34).

BLIND BARTIMAEUS: MARK 10:46–52

Here, following a section of teaching on a true understanding of discipleship in the light of the unfolding drama of the cross, Jesus is described as just about to leave Jericho on the final leg of his journey to Jerusalem. Bartimaeus, a blind beggar, knew of Jesus' reputation, and knew what he wanted, and no amount of rebukes or discouragement from the crowd would keep him silent (verse 48). Jesus 'heard' and summoned the man, who threw off his robe and ran forward, in significant contrast to the manner of the disciples making their way behind Jesus to Jerusalem (verse 32).

Once again I ask the question: 'What do we learn from this encounter about the listening of Jesus?'

- Jesus stood still (verse 49) – he literally stopped, when it would have been so easy, in the busyness of his day and the demands he was about to face in Jerusalem, to ignore this one voice among many.
- Jesus took Bartimaeus and his need seriously when others around clearly didn't.
- He allowed Bartimaeus freedom and space to exercise choice by asking what would have seemed to others an unnecessary question: 'What do you want me to do for you?' (verse 51).

- He is not told he is healed, but to 'Go, your faith has healed you' (verse 52).

As with all Jesus' healings, the man has not earned his cure, but in Mark's Gospel it is the response of faith commitment which provides the arena in which the drama of salvation takes place. As he goes, 'Immediately he received his sight, and followed Jesus along the road' (verse 52).

What is also clear from these two illustrations, and so many other examples of the Jesus who listens, is that in addition to hearing people's words, and their outward cries for help, he had the capacity to listen behind what was unsaid, including, where necessary, pointing out inconsistencies and challenging sinfulness (see Matthew 12:9–12; 15:1–9; Mark 12:13–17). Clearly his listening was of the 'double kind' that has been referred to earlier in the book, to people with their needs and problems as well, constantly turning back to listen to his Father; all evidence of a truly redemptive listening that enters into and takes to himself our needs and pain, our hopes and fears.

God has not only spoken through his Son. What is perhaps more important, he has listened through his Son. Christ's saving work cost him most in its speechless passivity or dereliction. It is this which gives him the right to be called the greatest listener to all suffering. It is this which gives his listening its redemptive quality.[3]

Select bibliography

Atkins, Martyn, *Resourcing Renewal,* Inspire, 2007

Belisle, Peter-Damian, *The Language of Silence,* Darton, Longman & Todd, 2003

Bochen, C. M., *Thomas Merton – Essential Writings,* Orbis Books, 2000

Bonhoeffer, Dietrich, *Life Together*, SCM, 1980

Bookless, Dave, *Planetwise*, IVP, 2008

Brueggemann, Walter, *Cadences of Home – Preaching Among Exiles*, Westminster John Knox, 1997

Bryant, Christopher, *The River Within*, Darton, Longman & Todd, 1978

Chambers, Oswald, *My Utmost for his Highest*, Discovery House, 1995

Coggan, Donald, *The Sacrament of the Word,* Collins Fount, 1987

Cottrell, Stephen, *Do Nothing to Change Your Life,* Church House Publishing, 2007

Cottrell, Stephen, *Hit the Ground Kneeling*, Church House Publishing, 2008

Cragg, Kenneth, *Sandals at the Mosque*, SCM, 1959

Croft, Steven, Freddy Hedley and Bob Hopkins, *Listening for Mission*, Fresh Expressions/ Church House Publishing, 2006

Donovan, Vincent, *Christianity Rediscovered*, SCM, 1984

Donovan, Vincent, *The Church in the Midst of Creation*, SCM, 1989

Duncan, Malcolm, *Kingdom Come*, Monarch, 2007

Dunn, Ronald, *When Heaven is Silent*, Nelson Word, 1994

Edmondson, Chris, *Minister, Love Thyself*, Grove Books, 2000

Edmondson, Chris, *Fit to Lead,* Darton, Longman & Todd, 2002

Finney, John, *The Well Church Book*, CPAS, 1991

Foster, Richard, *Celebration of Discipline*, Hodder & Stoughton, 1980

Foster, Richard, *Prayer*, Hodder & Stoughton, 1992

Goldsmith, Martin, *What About Other Faiths?*, Hodder & Stoughton, 2008

Greig, Pete, *God on Mute,* Survivor, 2007

Hall, Sister Jeremy, *Silence, Solitude, Simplicity*, Liturgical Press, 2007

Harper, Michael, *Let my People Grow*, Hodder & Stoughton, 1977

Hughes, Gerard, *Walk to Jerusalem*, Darton, Longman & Todd, 1991

Huggett, Joyce, *Learning the Language of Prayer*, BRF, 1994

Huggett, Joyce, *Open to God*, Hodder & Stoughton, 1984

Iles, Paul, *Touching the Far Corner,* Bible Society, 1996

Jackson, Gordon, *Wisdom for the Way*, NavPress, 2000

Jersak, Brad, *Can You Hear Me? Tuning In to the God Who Speaks*, Monarch, 2006

Kierkegaard, Soren, *Either/Or*, Princeton University Press, 1944

Kirkpatrick, Bill, *The Creativity of Listening*, Darton, Longman & Todd, 2005

Lewis, C. S., *A Grief Observed*, Bantam, 1976

Long, Anne, *Listening*, Darton, Longman & Todd, 1990

Maclaren, Brian, *The Church on the Other Side*, Zondervan, 2000

McGrath, Alister, *Christian Spirituality*, Blackwell, 1999

Merton, Thomas, *Confessions of a Guilty Bystander*, Image Books, 1968

Merton, Thomas, *No Man is an Island*, Burns and Oates, 1955

Merton, Thomas, *The Collected Poems of Thomas Merton*, New Directions, 1977

Mitton, Michael, *A Heart to Listen*, BRF, 2004

Mitton, Michael, *The Sounds of God*, Eagle, 1993

Murray, Stuart, *Post-Christendom: Church and Mission in a Strange New World,* Paternoster, 2004

Nee Watchman, *Sit, Walk, Stand*, Victory Press, 1957

Nouwen, Henri, *In the Name of Jesus: Reflections on Christian Leadership*, Darton, Longman & Todd, 1989

Nouwen, Henri, *Reaching Out*, Fount, 1974

Nouwen, Henri, *Out of Solitude*, Ave Maria Press, 1974

Nouwen, Henri, *The Way of the Heart,* Darton, Longman & Todd, 1981

O'Donovan, Oliver, *A Conversation Waiting to Begin*, SCM, 2009

Peace, Richard, *Spiritual Journalling*, NavPress, 1998

Peall, Gillian, *How Can I Hear God?*, Scripture Union, 2007

Percy, Martyn, *Clergy: The Origin of Species*, Continuum, 2006

Peterson, Eugene, *The Contemplative Pastor*, Eerdmans, 1989

Pritchard, John, *The Life and Work of a Priest*, SPCK, 2007

Runcorn, David, *The Road to Growth Less Travelled*, Grove Books, 2008

Runcorn, David, *Space for God*, Darton, Longman & Todd, 1990

Ryrie, Alexander, *Silent Waiting*, Canterbury Press, 1999

Stackhouse, Ian, *Gospel-driven Church*, Paternoster, 2004

Stewart, Columba, *Prayer and Community*, Darton, Longman & Todd, 1998

Thiselton, Anthony, *The First Epistle to the Corinthians: A Commentary on the Greek Text,* Paternoster, 2000

Waal, Esther de, *Living with Contradiction*, Collins Fount, 1989

Walker, Simon P., *Leading Out of Who You Are: Discovering the Secret of Undefended Leadership*, Piquant, 2007

Williamson, Tracy, *Letting God Speak Through You*, New Wine Press, 2006

Williamson, Tracy, *Expecting God to Speak to You*, New Wine Press, 2005

Wingate, Andrew, *Celebrating Difference, Staying Faithful*, Darton, Longman & Todd, 2005

Notes

Introduction

1 Nancy Kline, *Time to Think* (London: Ward Lock, 1999)
2 Donald Coggan, *The Sacrament of the Word* (London: Collins Fount, 1987), pp.31–32
3 *Foundation for Church Leadership Conference Booklet* (2005), p.5
4 Henri Nouwen, *In the Name of Jesus: Reflections on Christian Leadership* (London: Darton, Longman & Todd, 1989), pp.29–30

Chapter one

1 Vincent Donovan, *Christianity Rediscovered – An Epistle from the Masai* (London: SCM, 1982, and republished many times since)
2 Soren Kierkegaard, *Either/Or, Volume 1* (Princeton: Princeton University Press, 1944), p.66
3 *Cruden's Complete Concordance* (London: Hodder & Stoughton, 1990)
4 Bill Kirkpatrick, *The Creativity of Listening* (London: Darton, Longman & Todd, 2005), p.5
5 Stuart Murray, *Post-Christendom: Church and Mission in a Strange New World* (Carlisle: Paternoster, 2004), p.6
6 Martyn Atkins, *Resourcing Renewal* (Peterborough: Inspire, 2007), p.119
7 Andrew Wingate, *Celebrating Difference, Staying Faithful* (London: Darton, Longman & Todd, 2005)
8 See in particular Walter Brueggemann, *Cadences of Home: Preaching Among Exiles* (Louisville: Westminster John Knox, 1997)
9 Ibid. p.6
10 Malcolm Duncan, *Kingdom Come* (Oxford: Monarch, 2007), p.133

Chapter two

1 Dietrich Bonhoeffer, *Life Together* (London: SCM Press, 1980), p.76
2 T. S. Eliot, *Collected Poems, 1909–1962* (London: Faber and Faber, 1970), p.102
3 Michael Mitton, *The Wisdom to Listen* (Cambridge: Grove Books, 2002), p.7

4   John Sandford, *Ministry Burnout* (Evesham: Arthur James Books, 1982)

5   Tim Chester, *The Busy Christian's Guide to Busyness* (Leicester: IVP, 2006), pp.105–106

6   Bonhoeffer, *Life Together*, p.75

7   Stephen Cottrell, *Do Nothing to Change Your Life* (London: Church House Publishing, 2007), p.31

8   Quoted in Robert D. Putnam, *Bowling Alone: The Collapse and Revival of American Community* (New York: Simon and Schuster, 2000), p.189

9   Christopher Bryant, *The River Within* (London: Darton, Longman & Todd, 1978), p.73

10 Roy Oswald, *Clergy Self-care: Finding a Balance for Effective Ministry* (New York: Alban Institute, 1991), p.93

Chapter three

1   Quoted in *Wisdom for the Way*, compiled by Gordon S. Jackson (Colorado Springs: NavPress, 2000), p.123

2   Pete Greig, *God on Mute: Engaging the Silence of Unanswered Prayer* (London: Kingsway, 2007), p.237

3   Ibid. p.240

4   Quoted by Alister McGrath in *Christian Spirituality* (Blackwell: Oxford, 1999), pp.107–108

5   Eugene Peterson, *The Contemplative Pastor* (Grand Rapids: Eerdmans, 1989)

6   Ian Stackhouse, *The Gospel-driven Church* (Milton Keynes: Paternoster, 2005), p.227

7   Watchman Nee, *Sit, Walk, Stand* (London: Victory Press, 1957), p.13

8   Richard Foster, *Prayer* (London: Hodder & Stoughton, 1992), p.100

9   Quoted in *UK Focus*, August 2009, p.7

10 Quoted from an anonymous article, 'Egg-sucking for grandmothers: lesson one', *Church Times*, 21 August 2009

11 Simon P. Walker, *Leading Out of Who You Are: Discovering the Secret of Undefended Leadership* (Carlisle: Piquant, 2007), p.125

12 *Christianity and Renewal*, February 2001

13 Alexander Ryrie, *Silent Waiting* (London: Canterbury Press, 1999), p.164

14 Joyce Huggett, *Learning the Language of Prayer* (Oxford: BRF, 1994), p.42

15 John Pritchard, *The Life and Work of a Priest* (London: SPCK, 2007), p.103

16 Stephen Cottrell, *Hit the Ground Kneeling* (London: CHP, 2008), p.8

17 David Runcorn, *Space for God* (London: Daybreak, 1990), p.4

18 Ibid. pp.4–5

19 Henri Nouwen, *Out of Solitude* (New York: Ave Maria Press, 1974), p.56

20 From *When Lonely, A Book of Private Prayer*, quoted in Paul Iles, *Touching the Far Corner* (London: Bible Society, 1996)

21 Henri Nouwen, *The Way of the Heart* (London: Darton, Longman & Todd, 1981), p.27

22 Mother Teresa, *In the Silence of the Heart* (London: SPCK, 1983), p.19

23 Richard Peace, *Spiritual Journalling* (Colorado Springs: NavPress, 1998), pp.7, 10

24 Simon P. Walker, *Leading Out of Who You Are*, p.44

25 Thomas Merton, *No Man is an Island* (London: Burns and Oates, 1955), p.61

26 C. S. Lewis, *A Grief Observed* (New York: Bantam, 1976), pp.4–5

27 Oswald Chambers, *My Utmost for His Highest*, Special Updated Edition, ed. James Reimann (Grand Rapids: Discovery House, 1995), pp.10–11

28 Teresa of Avila, *The Interior Castle* (Stanbrook Abbey Press, 1663) ch. 31.2

29 Ibid. 31.3.

Chapter four

1 Quoted in Henri Nouwen, *Out of Solitude* (New York: Ave Maria Press, 1974), pp.14ff

2 Quoted in Joyce Huggett, *Open to God* (London: Hodder & Stoughton, 1984), p.81

3 Dave Bookless, *Planetwise* (Leicester: IVP, 2008), p.11

4 Martyn Percy, *Clergy: The Origin of Species* (London: Continuum, 2006), pp.108–109

5 Ibid. p.51

6 Quoted from an article in *UK Focus*, August 2009

7 *CR: Quarterly Review of the Community of the Resurrection*, Lady Day 2010 p.3

8 Oliver O'Donovan, *A Conversation Waiting to Begin* (London: SCM, 2009), p.49

9 GS 1577

10 Martin Goldsmith, *What About Other Faiths?* (London: Hodder & Stoughton, 2008), p.145

11 Kenneth Cragg, *Sandals at the Mosque* (London: SCM, 1959)

12 Oliver O'Donovan, *A Conversation Waiting to Begin*, pp.63, 69

13 Henri Nouwen, *Reaching Out* (London: Fount, 1974), quoted in Charles R. Forster, *Educating Christian Congregations: the Future of Christian Education* (Nashville: Abingdon Press, 1994), p.66

14 'The Listening Leader – stories of interfaith work in Bradford', *Leadership Review* No.2, FCL, 2008

15 *The Collected Poems of Thomas Merton* (New Directions: New York, 1977), p.380

16 Columba Stewart, *Prayer and Community* (London: Darton, Longman & Todd, 1998) p.28

17 *Lambeth Reflections*, p.76

18 Gerard Hughes, *Walk to Jerusalem* (London: Darton, Longman & Todd, 1991), quoted in Emmanuel Church, Loughborough's publicity for a course on Christian listening)

19 Oliver O'Donovan, *A Conversation Waiting to Begin*, p.119

20 ACC 3, 1976, p.55

Chapter five

1 John Pritchard, *The Life and Work of a Priest* (London: SPCK, 2007), p.131

2 John Pritchard, *The Life and Work of a Priest*, p.103

3 Ian Stackhouse, *Gospel-driven Church*, p.237

4 Quoted in Thomas Merton, *Confessions of a Guilty Bystander* (New York: Image Books, 1968), pp.44–45

5 Preface to the Argentine edition of *The Complete Works of Thomas Merton*, quoted in C. M. Bochen, *Thomas Merton – Essential Writings* (Maryknoll, New York: Orbis Books, 2000), p.16

6 Esther de Waal, *Living with Contradiction* (London: Collins Fount, 1989), p.115

7 David Runcorn, *The Road to Growth Less Travelled* (Nottingham: Grove Books, 2008), p.10

8 Ibid. p.21

9 Anthony Thiselton, *The First Epistle to the Corinthians: A Commentary on the Greek Text* (Carlisle: Paternoster, 2000), p.964

10 James D. G. Dunn, *Jesus and the Spirit: A Study of the Religious and Charismatic Experience of Jesus and the First Christians as Reflected in the New Testament* (Grand Rapids: Eerdmans, 1997), p.234

11 R. Collins, *First Corinthians* (Minnesota: Liturgical Press, 1999), p.455

12 Michael Harper, *Let My People Grow* (London: Hodder & Stoughton, 1977), p.51

13 John Pritchard, *The Life and Work of a Priest*, pp.93–4

14 Anne Long, *Listening* (London: Darton, Longman & Todd, 1990), p.71

15 Thomas R. Kelly, *A Testament of Devotion*, quoted by Richard Foster in *A Celebration of Discipline* (London: Hodder & Stoughton, 1980), p.40

16 John Finney, *The Well Church Book* (Warwick: CPAS, 1991), p.12

17 Ibid. p.95

Afterword

1 National Business Hall of Fame

2 Anne Long, *Listening*, p.175

3 Frank Lake, *Listening and Responding*, Clinical Theology Association pamphlet, p.30, B13

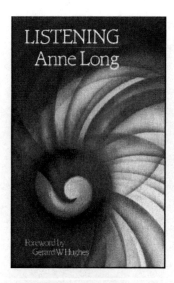